UNCOMMON AND UNFINISHED

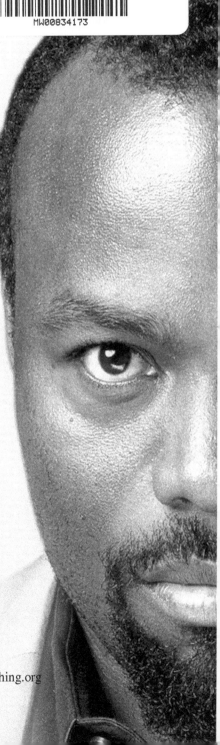

THE
BEN TROUPE
STORY

BEN TROUPE
WITH B.J. BENNETT

www.TrueVinePublishing.org

Uncommon and Unfinished
Ben Troupe with BJ Bennett

Published by True Vine Publishing Company
P.O. Box 22448, Nashville, TN 37202
www.TrueVinePublishing.org

ISBN: 978-1-7366672-8-6
Copyright © 2021 by Ben Troupe and BJ Bennett

Printed in the United States of America—First Printing

To place orders for more books or to book the author for speaking engagements, visit: www.BenTroupe84.com

DEDICATION

Daddy, thank you for showing me the way of never giving up and never giving in. Mama, thank you for being everything that I needed, even when I wasn't ready to accept it or receive it. Nikki and Lucus, thank y'all for being my left and right side. Carianna, thank you for being my inspiration.

B.J., thank you for being my prince and my legacy. Yaya and Mia, thank y'all for being my heart, my smile, my joy, my life and my everything. Rian, Jalin, Jamie, Julian, Christian, Kierston and Josh, thank y'all for helping me be the most blessed uncle in the world.

To my friends and teammates and the cities of Swainsboro, Augusta, Gainesville, Nashville, Tampa and Oakland, thank you for grooming me, shaping me and giving me my voice, my platform and my purpose.

TABLE OF CONTENTS

FOREWORD

Foreword by Antre' Drummer
Associate Tenured Professor of Mathematics
Director of the African American Male Initiative
(AAMI) East Georgia State College

Ben Troupe, former NFL tight end and All-American Florida Gator great, is the personification of the phrase "give back". When I met Mr. Ben Troupe, I met a kindred spirit indeed. Ben would say, "I met a brother, and the root of brother is 'other', and I just met my other brother, that's all." Ben immediately took interest in my work with the *African American Male Initiative* (AAMI), a program designed to help African American males navigate college. "What can I do to help these men?" was the question Ben asked when we first met. Our bond was solidified right then. We continue to be focused on changing the negative, dilapidated narrative of African American males. Our intertwined visions opened opportunities for me to further discover who Ben Troupe really is.

I've learned that Ben Troupe was born to exceed the ordinary and make the extraordinary his normal. Ben is known for his outstanding athletic abilities, but I've come to know the Father, the Brother, the Uncle and the Son. These titles are purposefully capitalized because they are serious titles to Ben. He has routinely stated, "a title without taking on the responsibility of the title profits nothing."

There is no distance too far and no journey too great for Ben. It is vitally important to him that any man carrying a title shows himself present. Ben Troupe is present in all facets of his being. I'm telling you that which I have witnessed. Being in Ben's presence brings out the best in you, it makes you dig deeper. It forces you to examine yourself and show gratitude to others in far greater ways than one could ever imagine. He is a firm believer in being 'thou brother's keeper.' Ben believes we don't get from ordinary to extraordinary on our own. In this life, if we're going to do great things, "it is not a me thing, it's a we thing."

Ben Troupe is a man of his word. I am delighted to be recognized as one of his "other brothers". Ben Troupe is next level greatness. I have no doubt that after reading this book, you will desire to search yourself to determine if you have truly been grateful for every person and opportunity that you have been given. You will desire to search yourself to determine if you have honored those who have routinely poured into your life. You will long to "give back" to your communities, because you will realize just how much has been given to you. I have no doubt that you will discover exactly who Mr. Ben Troupe really is.

FOUNDATIONS

PROMISED MY DAD I WOULD NEVER END UP IN JAIL.

Though much of my adult life has been spent in the spotlight, the shadows have often been where my mind has wandered. Shadows come in many different forms. Growing up, I compared mine to my father's and mine to my older brother's, just as young kids often do. As I aged, however, I started to learn more about a more intimidating shade: the gloom of incarceration. It's one that can come in many forms.

At first, prison was a simple reality for me. I spent so much time there, visiting my dad, that it never really felt out of place. Some children went to the park with their pops; I went to the penitentiary, instead. With time, I started to learn more about the dark, dreary cells where numbers replace names. These were places I couldn't go with my father, wouldn't go to mentally and tried hard not to imagine my dad in. Within all of this obscurity, I learned lessons that weren't initially clear. I was ultimately discovering who I was. I was also establishing both who I did and did not want to be.

Even in the darkest of places, a flicker in my father's eyes has long come with a broader illumination. I still chase that light to this day. It's a road, headlights peering through a dimming dusk, I'm still on.

Who I am is a story that starts in Swainsboro, Georgia. It's a winding tale told more in small towns like Twin

City, Vidaila and Wadley than in metropolitan areas like Nashville, Oakland or Tampa Bay. Well before Gainesville, even, there was Midville. Each of those map dots were places I traveled through on countless occasions to see my dad, John Wesley Troupe, while he was behind bars. Oftentimes more than once. The criminal justice system was a normal part of my childhood. Visitations were our family vacations.

Traveling from facility to facility, I learned the backroads of Georgia long before I would ever drive them. I grew up where others were locked up. With how common these experiences were for me and my siblings, I never even knew the difference at first. While others saw perpetrators in those tight, nondescript rooms, I simply saw people.

Not once, as a very small child at least, did I feel uncomfortable or out of place. In rooms with no windows, I couldn't see what was outside anyway. I didn't want to. I didn't need to. I only saw who was right in front of me: a man I still call "Daddy".

As a kid, I looked forward to these visits. It was routine for extended family to come with us. We even celebrated birthdays on prison grounds, sharing memories mere feet from where so many others were being sadly forgotten. We were definitely counting the years, just not the same way as everybody else.

One of my favorite childhood parties was held at the prison facility in Springfield. Other prisoners actually helped set up the festivities and pass out the cake. I originally felt right at home behind bars. After all, my daddy was there. As I got older, I became determined not to make that a habit.

There were then two sides to Daddy, who wavered between being two men. Both of his examples came with an education no school could ever provide. Like any young boy in awe of their daddy's seemingly-unrelenting strength and savvy, I grew up idolizing the one who made me. Countless stories of my daddy stirred my early imagination, especially those he, charismatic in his delivery and strong in his convictions, glowingly told himself. There has always been a magic to this hulking man, his bold personality making him a local legend.

My daddy's early reputation across east Georgia was somewhat of a contradiction; he was the same man you would go to for help and, during the rough stretches of his life, the same man who would go looking for a fix. Though I didn't always know it, the perception of my daddy often ebbed and flowed between fellowship and fear. This man of faith sometimes lost his direction, trying his best to remain steadfast through wherever he stumbled. My father has always been himself to a fault, beholden to his feelings and stubborn in seeing them through.

Daddy does everything with all that he has. That passion, when misguided, almost cost him his life. Your biggest strength can sometimes be your biggest weakness. That balance is one daddy has sometimes struggled to find.

John always had the drive and motivation to get whatever he wanted. He married my mother as a wide-eyed teenager without much money to his name, guiding her into the future with that very same promise of persistence. It's one, through good times and bad for my parents, that remains honest and authentic over 40 years later. Daddy's core has always been one of love; it's how that commitment has manifested itself that has sometimes dramatically changed.

Daddy's legacy, today, is one of leadership. Not far from the very same streets he used to terrorize and wreak havoc on, Daddy now walks tall through those neighborhoods with a very different purpose. He is the CEO of a faith-based community initiative, the grizzled face of Men Reaching Men, a non-profit organization that brings men of all ages together to discuss social issues, establish volunteer programs and mentor many in underserved areas.

Group members also support each other as well. Daddy has war stories that still need to be heard and shared. Echoes from yesteryear will always be part of who he is. That said, my daddy has tirelessly fought for the position he is now in. When this voice tells others there is a better way, those words come with and from experience.

What is interesting to think about, with regards to my daddy, is that he and I both have gone through meaningful reintroductions. We have had to get to know each other time and time again. It hasn't always worked. Just as Daddy had to start over from scratch, I have had to in my own way. Being a football player comes with certain stigmas and perceptions. I constantly have to overcome the initial assumptions of others. Folks judge my daddy off of what they have heard. They judge me off of what they have seen.

Together, we are tearing down the walls of false narratives. I have taken the time and made it a point to learn everything there is to know about my daddy. His story is one that shapes me. His story is one I share.

Daddy, rough and tumble, proudly joined the United States Army at a young age and, just ask around, was a bonafide basketball legend on the Texas courts of Fort Hood. He remains one of the best players to ever come through east Georgia, a former star at Swainsboro High School. Ask my father, now limited by back injuries that have come from decades of puck-wooding, about his game and he will respond with a laugh and a wink. On the right day, however, he might even give you a wince and a dusty jump shot, one with the same sweet follow-through.

Even as he ages, parts of Daddy remain forever frozen in time. The wrinkles on his brow connect proverbial dots and paint quite the picture. Every single one of them are well-earned. Each line on this man's face forms roots that run deep. You can call Daddy living history. When he talks, I still hear his dad Clifford in his voice. Despite my late grandfather barely standing over five feet tall, the respect he commanded and the knowledge he had remains a family and community benchmark. Young ones in the family don't even realize how much of Clifford exists in them.

The exact same goes for my grandmother Mollie. They were a powerful duo. Quite the pair around town. Together, they were a proud and confident bunch, with a strength they found and fostered in each other. Daddy's parents grew old in an old-fashioned manner, with values firmly in place. Their base was rock-solid, even when the dust gathered and the weeds grew. That simplicity gave me the courage and freedom to find my own way. Sometimes, that direction was just me running wild.

Like many families in the Deep South, my grandparents lived out in the country. Their place was the kind of place you had a hard time explaining to strangers how to get to. That said, most everybody around town knew the land like the back of their hand. Grandma and Granddaddy's home was one where their yard simply blended into the surrounding woods nearby. They had a gruff collection of mutts and farm animals that were always somewhere around. Dogs and chickens sometimes came and went like people.

One of the leading memories my brother and I have seared into our brains from sun-scorched time outside at Clifford and Mollie's was the fear of the "super roosters". They ruled this part of Swainsboro. I am far from an expert on farmland zoology, how these creatures evolved or where they came from; all I know is that if these super roosters showed up for 4th grade math class, they would be taller than every single student in the room.

Clifford and Mollie's super roosters were half-chicken, half-TV villain; think a more evil version of Foghorn Leghorn, with dark feathers and a bold soul. Strange things happen in the backwoods and these birds were the ultimate feathery example. Lucus and I grew up fleeing from them and, later, having to face our fears and fight them. When he and I were kids, we would have sudden stand-offs at the *O.K. Corral*, with our wide eyes meeting their beady ones and deep uncertainty settling in. These super roosters could sense fear. They could smell it.

Years before I played the South Carolina Gamecocks, they were a foe I knew all too well. Maybe these super roosters were the first Coastal Carolina Chanticleers.

As with any other obstacle, Daddy was always there to see us through. His valiant glare somehow seemed to silence the super roosters, even their strong and ferocious leader "Big Red". When Daddy wasn't there, his presence still remained and resonated, giving us strength in this epic territorial clash. Lucus and I needed our hero to pull us through. Daddy's presence still calms my nerves to this day.

For my father's sooty exterior, always coming home literally covered in the hard work he constantly did, his heart has always been one of gold. Love, mind you, is the greatest form of strength. From my mother always standing by daddy's side, to his path always returning back to her, our house full of athletes and soldiers and farmers and prisoners has forever been one where the foundation hasn't and won't ever change.

Faith and family stand the test of time. While Lucus, our sister Nikki and I are all within a few years of age, our younger sister Carianna is over a decade younger. There is a reason for that beyond just time. A generation ago, we went to pick up our new baby cousin to spend some time with her and give our extended family members a short break. We always made it a point to visit with our aunts, uncles and cousins and this trip was no different. This particular weekend, though, turned into a lifetime.

My parents, upon picking Carianna up, immediately felt a connection. We all did. She fit our family perfectly and seemed like the long-lost frame that finally put our full picture together. A few days turned into a few weeks. As circumstances were, Carianna's stay with us became an extended one. My parents were given the opportunity to raise her as their own and, without hesitation, did just that.

Carriana's upbringing hasn't been any different as she is the beloved baby of not just our family, but the entire Troupe tree. All of us have different stories, but we all have the same last name. That tie is forever binding.

Beyond my mama and just us kids, Daddy has always had an affinity for people. He is the type of man who can walk into a room and become the center of attention without ever saying a word. When he does speak, what he says matters. There were a lot of times in our relationship, those when Daddy was struggling, when he and I didn't talk much. Those stretches left a gaping void in my life. I was forced to fill them with assumptions.

When I talk to Daddy now, I do so with an appreciation for all that he has done: the good, the bad and the indifferent. How we see things is the first part of how we process them. I now understand that every step of my daddy's life has led him to where he currently is. Progress made has been difficult and deliberate. After all, nothing worth doing is ever easy.

One of the great benefits of my early childhood, and one of the great testaments to my mama, Cheryl Denise Troupe, was that my environment remained stable and warm even when chaos swirled. I was blessed to be raised in a garden of good, one with rich black soil and sunshine. Within walking distance of my childhood home were countless relatives, loving caretakers who groomed and cultivated me into the man I am today.

While the world was enamored with the technological boom of the 1990s, I could stand in my backyard and yell loud enough to reach many of the people who meant the most to me. There was comfort in those close surroundings. Like tomatoes on a wire, I blossomed from there.

That proud simplicity came with practical applications. Clifford and Mollie's home was nestled on a dirt road in a setting that belonged in *Little House on the Prairie*. Their structure was a tin-roofed cabin with limited electricity and no running water. And super roosters scheming outside. It was there, with my daddy's mother and father, that I spent many of my summer days.

Activities that now seem as outdated as black-and-white television, we built forts, climbed trees and dug holes. We played with dogs and, yes, ran from super roosters. We rubbed red clay on open cuts. We said "sir" and "ma'am" and understood what might happen if we didn't. And it wasn't timeout or restriction, either.

While there was everything we needed inside the house, everything else took place outside the house; as in a literal out-house. When folks asked where the bathroom was, we just pointed to the yard. All of this was part of me learning to make the abnormal normal, the uncomfortable comfortable.

Mollie was the matriarch of the family and, in some ways, one of the leaders of all of Swainsboro. It was she who constantly reinforced the idea of family. Her suggestions and servings always came with seconds and thirds. From older relatives to the children alike, food was and remains one joy that has always brought us all together. Some family heads rule with an iron fist. Mollie ruled with an iron ladle.

From mashed potatoes and gravy to macaroni and cheese and greens, her meals were burn-your-mouth good. In the black community, we use the same word twice when something is really good; my grandma could cook-cook. And Mollie, somehow, always had more than enough for everybody. A whole football team if need be. The servings, just like her love, always kept coming. She was the grandmother from the movie *Soul Food* and taught us that family was all we ever needed.

It's been said that it takes a village to raise a child and that was certainly the case with my crew. Mollie had a school bus full of children, my father John, Clifford and Robert included, but she cared for all of the cousins and kids as if they were her own. Whether her own children or other growing babies like Carla, Cola, Dana, Josh, Ki-wame, Leddy, Lil' Rico, Lil' Robert or myself, Mollie always found a way to make room. We listened to her, learned from her and loved her.

Though modest, Mollie and Clifford's home was a house of sheer fulfillment and joy. On Sundays after church, it served as the center of the world, lines out the door and all.

Memories of us talking and laughing, joking and singing, still echo in my mind. So do my grandma's old sayings, bursts of originality that didn't always make sense to me at the time. She had an especially affectionate way of saying "shut-tup", pronouncing the letter "t" two different times. She was really good at doing impressions also and could actually do a great Dean Martin. Simply put, she was a person who nobody wanted to leave. Her house was a magnet on an old refrigerator, this one always pulling us all back home.

From Mollie to my great-grandmother Neloise, aka "Babychild", and my grandmother Cora Bell on my mama's side, I was blessed to grow up in a world of absolute wisdom. So many of their perspectives were sewn in a simpler time, with a focus on the fundamentals that I miss. There were simple pleasures, like taking coins down to the corner store, which were often makeshift setups in the living rooms of others, for candy.

Decades later, I still remember the comfort of going to sleep with the rain distinctly hitting a rusty tin roof. In some ways, those thumps were one-and-the-same with the beats in my chest. I miss those moments. Like a slice of sweet potato pie, I crave them in today's non-stop traffic and noise.

The scene was roughly the same all over town. Given where and when I was a grade-schooler, we were some of the last kids to truly grow up outside. I am thankful for that. I cherish those memories. We hopped from house to house like frogs on lily pads, my cousins and I racing street to street. Whether it was the porches of extended family or places owned by Jimmy Dales, Charles Martin, Ms. Dollie, Ms. Pearl or the Gillis Store, every stop felt the same to me: like home. Imagine that.

In a very real sense, the beauty of a place like Swainsboro is how your story is also someone else's. Here was my first, and most important, huddle. While our homes may have been small, our community came with all we ever needed. Whether a meal or a mend, others were always there for us. It was a "least among us" mentality that resonated with and inspired me.

Growing up, every friend I had went to Feed-A-Kid in the summer. In the school year, we all leaned in to learn more from our bus drivers, legendary characters like Jack Bright, Ollie, and Pudge. We all played rec-league sports and we all did so for the same people; if you are from Swainsboro, you remember Mr. Woody Nasworthy, Mr. Carmichael and Miss Connie with her white visor. We didn't use Google Maps to pick a playground, we all went to the exact same one.

Life was easy to come by and love was, too. Just about anything I wanted as a child could be gotten with a quick sprint down the road and a quarter or two. If one family member told me no, there was always another one to ask right around the corner. The fact that the rest of the world wasn't always this way came as a shocking surprise to me as I aged and expanded out. I am deeply appreciative of all that I have gotten to do, but part of me misses the Swainsboro of my youth and always will.

My honest, humble beginnings showed me what was important and ultimately taught me how to handle some of the fortune and fame that later came. Without that exact start, I'm not sure there would have been a similar finish. Me overcoming adversity, attending college and ultimately playing at football's highest level all got started long before. The Ben Troupe that *was* created opportunities for the Ben Troupe that *is*. Even when he didn't know it.

My frame of reference was never that wide, an out-look that proved important as my horizons opened up beyond my wildest imagination. A small circle and simple scope helped me maintain my balance as I sprinted into adulthood. I have accomplished all that I set out to do as a young man and have done so without ever compromising my principles. That process, through it all, is what I am most proud of.

From a young age, we shared everything in Swainsboro, including each other's successes. When I ran onto the field at the University of Florida and, after being selected 40th overall in the 2004 NFL Draft, debuted at the next level, I did so with family and friends right behind me. I received my draft-day call from the Tennessee Titans, actually on the phone of a cherished family friend, while standing not far from where my siblings and I went to daycare and my family and I went to church. The people who heard my cries as a baby were the same who saw me cry my tears of joy a generation later.

I walked the same uneven roads as a poor kid that I did as a suddenly-wealthy man. I'm forever thankful for the fact that my first moments after making it to the NFL were spent in the one place in the world that I wanted to be: a small town of roughly 7,000 people, just about every single one of whom knew me, my family or our name. I have heard others talk about how they went to a big city or fancy party after hearing their names called in the draft. If it's any consolation to them, Swainsboro was called Paris upon incorporation in 1854.

One of my favorite memories from those days is me and my cousin John-John driving over to Statesboro to help me pick out something to wear for my introductory press conference the next day in Nashville. My deep and sincere hope is that Swainsboro, along with Augusta, my other home, feel a sense of accomplishment over all that we did and all that we are still doing.

Swainsboro is the type of place where no introductions are ever needed. We knew other people by their people. Before I was Ben, I was "one of them Troupe boys", just like my brother Lucus. I always heard, "You're a Troupe, right?" and still do. To some people, that is exactly who I always will be, a notion I celebrate and embrace. My hometown sees me just as they see my family. I wouldn't have it any other way. Learning to walk to the years when I will one day struggle to, those in Swainsboro, Augusta, Vidalia and small towns in between, have always supported me.

These are places where neighborhoods replace names. A familiar face is what you know and trust. Even still, friends like "Dizzle", "Gator" and "Hot Rod" make up my personal inner-circle, with others like "Beaver Dog", "Bird Dog" and "Walk-A-Do" standing as folks I know around town. If some of them handed me a signed check with their legal name on it, I wouldn't know who it was from. Their handshakes and head-nods were all I ever needed. Nicknames, where I'm from, are your name.

Every place I have gone, that same mindset has come with me. Simply put, Swainsboro, just like for Titus Peebles, Charles Silas and Shannon Wadley, is where it all began. Titus, who played football at Arkansas, and Charles and Shannon, who both played at South Carolina, lived in the same neighborhood as my grandmother Cora

Bell. In that span of maybe a few dozen houses, DeAlva, located right down the road from the tallest basketball goals in the continental United States, four future SEC football players learned the same life lessons.

Shannon's mother, Ms. Phyllis, is a local legend, the owner and operator of Kiddie Kampus. If you were a little black kid who went to daycare in Swainsboro, that is where you got started.

Though we all went on to great gridiron success, I always envied Titus, Charles, Shannon and countless other children my age. As long as I can remember, all I ever wanted to be was a Swainsboro Tiger football player. Yes, I am incredibly proud to have played for the mighty Florida Gators, the Tennessee Titans, the Tampa Bay Buccaneers, the Oakland Raiders and the Butler High School Bulldogs. But my first goal was to suit up for Swainsboro. In my young eyes, they were the biggest names in town.

Charles, Titus, Brandon Andrews, Damian Coleman and Jason Samples were among those who led the team to an iconic state championship in 2000. While a later move to Augusta resulted in me graciously attending Butler, playing with the likes of future Auburn star, Thorpe Award winner, first round NFL Draft pick and Pro Bowler Carlos Rogers and former FCS All-American Isaac West, who finished as Furman's all-time leader in receptions and receiving yards, a younger me will always dream of kicking off weekends with a paw on the sides of my helmet.

Well before Saturday or Sunday, Friday night was all I could think about. After all, I had a legacy to uphold. Beyond my daddy's athletic achievements were those of my Uncle Robert. Before he went on to play quarterback at Fort Valley State University, Robert was a record-setting signal caller for those Swainsboro Tigers. Stories of him still make the rounds.

There remain times where I'm around town and people approach me with opinions that start with, "You were a great player, but your Uncle Robert...". If you see Robert and even make a mere reference to the game of football, the end result, whether he knows you or not, will be him reaching for your arm to show you the proper mechanical motion for the perfect downfield throw. And you better be paying attention. Still quick and strong, not to mention confident and eager, Robert will never be that far removed from the player so many still remember.

Suiting up for the Tigers, in one sport or another, is a tried-and-true family tradition. Though I'm thankful for the turns my life took, a big part of me will always be a hometown kid. Every game I played, every message I deliver as a public speaker, comes straight from Lincoln Street. Some of my recent work has allowed me to travel across the country and speak to businesses and colleges of notable esteem, the great University of You-Know-Who included.

Few experiences have topped my recent chance to talk to the Swainsboro boys basketball team before their 2019-2020 state championship game. They won, adding to the pride this professional still feels. That triumph, much like the football team's title in 2000 and a previous boys basketball championship in 1996, was one for the entire community. Within those news clippings are the stories of entire families. My late cousin Chico Washington is considered one of the greatest players in program history.

Though he was tragically killed in a shooting, Chico's son Chico, Jr. was on the recent title team. Chico's younger brother Sergio, Chico Jr.'s uncle, was the '96 title team.

Black, white or any shade in between, everybody in my town is black and gold. I may walk around with an NFL career on my resume, but those state title rings truly stand out. Folks at Maryland's Fried Chicken might one day think of people like me, but they will never forget 1996, 2000 or 2020.

Well before Titus earned his hardware, he and I grew up together, chasing the exact same goals and girls. One of my best childhood friends, someone I consider a brother, Titus went on to play alongside future NFL All-Pro Jason Peters at Arkansas. First, though, he and I waded through the same muck and mud.

Some of the most trouble I ever got into as a child came when Titus and I were swimming in a drainage ditch in the middle of a striking rain storm. Quickly, a puddle became a pool. Given that I was terribly afraid of thunderstorms growing up, this situation was one that sticks with me. The clouds were dark and deep, the lightning was close and crisp. That may have been the first time in my life I experienced true fear. It was Titus who was right there by my side.

Titus and I remained close up through me moving to Augusta and beyond. His mother, Pastor Christine Peeples, is the head of my family worship center, Victory Temple Church of Reconciliation, and a cherished friend and advisor. He and she both have helped me find my way when my steps have gone awry. Sister Chris, who always bought two blocks of cheese when she went to the store, one for her and one for me, is one of the people most responsible for my perspective on life. She showed me how and why it is important to be there for others.

Sister Chris also helped me understand that "to much is given, much is required". She also used to always tell me to "be encouraged!", a positive ideal that I continue to cling to. It was Sister Chris, in fact, who gave me the phone I used on NFL Draft day. The Tennessee Titans called her to call me. I see a lot of my mama in Titus' mother. Just about every single day they, with Sister Emma and Sister Amanda, are together in prayer at their home away from home. That strength is my strength. Their prayers changed everything and still do.

As was the case with my daddy, each and every one of my experiences have mattered. I will always have a longing for Swainsboro and I will always have an appreciation for Augusta. It was my foreign land in the very same state. My move to the southside, with Mama attending Augusta State, was my introduction to real life. I was getting older, had some actual responsibilities and had a new way of life to understand across the board. The transition was not an easy one. Daddy was gone, starting to succumb to his temptations and was struggling with addiction. Our mother was often alone.

My brother and sisters and I were adjusting to the idea of being around strangers, having to make new friends and, when the situation called for it, having to fend for ourselves. Times were tough, especially with the head of the household missing for days or weeks at a time. Above all else, Augusta was big. I was used to a town where my last name was good enough for credit at the local store, not one where nobody knew me or my family or seemed to even care.

In Swainsboro, the main street in town is literally called "Main Street" and it's a two-lane road. In Augusta, they had more traffic in one Wal-Mart. There, with Mama desperately trying to make ends meet and provide for us with Daddy more and more out of the picture, is where she worked. Meanwhile, we were sometimes forced to figure it all out alone.

Our move to Augusta found me, Lucus and Nikki in Williamsburg Apartments off Milledgeville Road. The complex was nothing like I had ever seen before, with more people than all of the neighborhoods of my childhood combined. In the area, there were gangs, drugs and guns. It felt like violence was everywhere. While time after school in Swainsboro was spent visiting friends and family, time after school in Augusta was spent wishing we were. We had to be strong.

Lucus and I, especially, were introduced to bullies. Though we tried to creep out of sight and mind our own business, fights were commonplace. One of my first memories of Augusta was Lucus getting choked by another kid in front of me and an onlooking crowd. We all felt helpless. It was shocking and startling to see. After that introduction to our new, dangerous reality, Lucus, who was making eye contact with me during all of this, made up in his mind that nobody was going to put their hands on him or his family ever again. The process was what it was. It made Lucus who he is.

I love Augusta, Nikki still lives in the area and it's a place that I value and cherish. Our start in the city, though, was nowhere near what we expected. Especially without Daddy around. Augusta, for me, took the training wheels off. Like Lucus, I had to respond and I did.

Life has a way of taking unexpected twists and turns, sometimes right up the road via Highway 56 and US 25-North. If you're lucky, you get a chance to come back home again. If you're really lucky, you get two homes along the way. People tell me that I've gotten the chance to do a lot of incredible things during my life, opportunities most could only dream of. I've been blessed, sure, but not just for the reasons outsiders think.

I've been shown the way by a father who took every possible turn. I've been inspired by a mother who never once turned her back. I've revered a brother serving overseas as a United States Marine. I've been amazed watching one sister earn a Master's Degree and another grow into a woman in her own unique way. I've seen a town love a family and that same family learn to love another town. I've seen so many impossible realities in my life. Very few of them came while wearing a helmet.

My life became a public one when I signed to play football at the University of Florida and, more so, when I was later drafted to play in the NFL. My story started long before. I needed my upbringing to later reach my full potential in adulthood. I don't think there is any way I could have had one without the other. Each one of my steps, from the former to the latter, has been made with a specific purpose in mind. The older I get, the more each stride starts to lead down a more meaningful path. It's one filled with friends and family.

On Thursday, February 27th, 2020, right before the tragic Covid-19 pandemic hit with full force, I kicked off my "Uncommon" Speaking Tour at East Georgia College in Swainsboro. As I stepped into the spotlight of that auditorium stage, my life had officially come full circle. I shared my memories, the good ones and the bad, with hundreds of people who both knew me and, prior to that night, probably thought that they did. I talked for over an hour, thanking local residents for their support and telling them just how much they all meant to me. It was a truly emotional event.

In addition to speaking directly to many family and friends, my goal was to influence the younger students on campus as well. Among them were leaders from the school's African American Male Initiative, an organization led by professor Antre' Drummer. I saw much of myself in many of them and made it a point to look them directly in the eyes when I talked. When they stood and clapped at the end of the evening, they saw my daddy and I on stage standing side-by-side.

Leading up to that night, I had the opportunity to stop and visit a few different places, all of which meant a lot to me. I spent the morning at the Swainsboro Alternative School, speaking to younger students about the importance of good decision-making and the far-reaching impact their choices can have. I told them about their immeasurable value and how absolutely important it was for them to reach and realize their full potential. I told them how much I was rooting for them and supporting them, even from afar.

I also warned them that going down the wrong path could one day lead them to a nearby place that they didn't want to go. It was a place, despite never being incarcerated, I knew all too well.

Mere hours later I was behind those very bars at the Emanuel County Jail, moving cell-block to cell-block while sharing the exact same message with the exact same people I warned the students about. The setting, in rooms with no color and dim light, was direct, honest and real. I spoke with conviction and courage, inspired by all that I had seen and experienced myself. After each session, there were handshakes and hugs, a look in the eyes of men who knew in their hearts that something had to give.

As I walked through those halls, I did so knowing that Daddy had spent countless days in environments just like this. I also remembered how important it was to him that I never stayed in a facility like the one I was in. Iron ominously clanking and closing behind me, I thought about Daddy's wishes and the promise I made to him years ago as I walked out of the building. Leaving a place where my father had spent many nights, this time I walked out with him. I didn't have to sign any papers or write any checks, either.

Pursuing our respective callings, Daddy and I shuffled our way through the jail parking lot together. Looking back as we left the facility, we, feeling a bond that had sometimes been missing, both looked forward as well.

ORANGE AND BLUE SKIES FOREVER

It's rare for a player from a town in the Peach State to turn down a chance to play football at the University of Georgia. In my case, I turned down the Bulldogs from two. My decision to sign with the University of Florida was one of the best decisions of my life. I remain thankful for the opportunity I received every single day. Though it was a difficult choice to turn down programs like Clemson, Louisville, North Carolina, South Carolina and UGA, which were some of my other favorites, my time in Gainesville was truly transformative. It was more than I ever could have imagined. I say that not just referencing the field or the classroom, but the community as well.

I felt at home in Gainesville and still do. If I ultimately became a man in Nashville, I started nudging in that general direction about 600 miles to the south. I learned about life, learned about personal responsibility and learned the business of college football. I also learned invaluable lessons like patience and perseverance, hard work, dedication and teamwork, and the significance of everything I did being about so much more than just me. I learned how to grind. I learned how to thrive. I learned how to endure. I also, like many young men who have had their eyes opened on campus, learned about women.

The irony of me signing with Florida, and the biggest play of my life coming against Georgia in Jacksonville, goes all of the way back to the end of my prep career and the transition from Butler High School to the next level. The first official pass I caught after signing my letter of intent wasn't from Rex Grossman, Chris Leak or Jesse Palmer, it was from Bulldog legend David Greene. And it was part of a game-winner. And it came, believe it or not, with me wearing red-and-black, against, of all opponents, Team Florida.

One of my favorite contests I ever played in was the Florida-Georgia All-Star Game in June of 2000. It was the very first time that I suited up after high school. Though we were all just pounds of potential at that point, the sheer talent on that field was absolutely unbelievable. Hosted at Georgia Tech's Bobby Dodd Stadium in Atlanta, this annual tradition was a rite of passage for top prospects in the Peach and Sunshine States. On my Georgia side, players included David and I, Ronnie Brown, Keyaron Fox, Travis Harris, Sean Jones, Kelvin Kight, Reshard Lee and others. Florida's roster had Eric Moore, Max Starks, Reggie Vickers and Vince Wilfork, among others.

First played in 1985 on a day where the iconic Deion Sanders starred, countless legends took part in this series. Names like Derrick Brooks, Daunte Culpepper, Troy Davis, Tommie Frazier, Jacquez Green, Garrison Hearst, John Kasay, Jamal Lewis, Warren Sapp, Fred Taylor and Charlie Ward are all part of its proud history. I'm honored and humbled to have played a very small role in it as well.

Late in our game, David, cool under pressure as always, found me on a shallow cross for an important two-point conversion. Our score gave Team Georgia a six-point win. Here is why that is now so fascinating. You simply can't make this stuff up. Just over two years later, I was obviously a junior tight end at Florida as we played

Georgia in Jacksonville. The game was a defensive slug-fest, with our two offenses struggling to make big plays.

Early in the fourth quarter, Rex Grossman threw me the most important ball of all that ever came my way. We were trailing 13-12, the outcome was very much in the balance and the eventual Heisman Trophy runner-up lofted me a perfect pass over the outstretched arms of future NFL All-Pro Thomas Davis. I was exhausted, honestly detached from the exact circumstances of the moment, yet somehow caught the pass to ultimately help us pull off the upset.

The final score, with me making a play for Florida to beat Georgia this time, was 20-13, a seven-point win. Many of the same guys I played with in the bi-state all-star game were right there on the sidelines that Saturday. Like me, Harris and Kight were first on that victorious Team Georgia before later helping the Gators get it done. When I sit and think about my life, it's parallels like those that often make me pause. Both times, I helped the good guys win.

That sequence, with at least half of the stadium screaming "TROOOUUUPE", or maybe it was the other side booing, became the signature play of my career. I still get asked about it nearly 20 years later.

I still think about it, too. Nobody, not even the guys in our huddle, knew just how completely drained I was before that play. If you go watch the highlight, I don't even celebrate after the touchdown. I run to the sidelines, take my helmet off and sit down. The excitement that surrounded that play was for everybody else. I was merely grateful I didn't fall down while running the route or drop the pass. Fear can be the best motivator.

Somehow, I wasn't aware of the sheer significance of what had just happened. It really hit me when I was interviewed after the game and a reporter asked me, a reserve tight end, a question I was totally unprepared to answer: how did it feel to catch the game-winning pass in the Florida-Georgia game? Though I had technically already done it once before, I still didn't know how to reflect on such a statement. All I wanted to do was win.

As is the case with every play, so much went into all that actually occurred. Our star wide receiver Taylor Jacobs got injured early, so we sort of had to adjust on the fly in the most important game of the year. Ed Zaunbrecher, our offensive coordinator, started to dictate tempo and spread the field. Before the game, we felt like that was our best chance to move the football against Georgia. We ran lots of bubble screens and tried to create favorable matchups for our playmakers in space. We started having some success.

Rex Grossman actually threw the football 46 times, with Kelvin Kight and Carlos Perez combining for 21 catches. On our final scoring drive, I emerged as a top target for one of the first times in my career. On third down in the redzone, against one of the most talented defenses and defenders I have ever faced, I got my chance to make a big play. I thank God that I did.

Georgia, trying to make us earn it as we neared the endzone, was in an aggressive cover zero scheme. It was every man for himself and I was matched up with one of the best and most athletic players in the country in Thomas Davis, a guy who would go on to help revolutionize professional defenses and become a Walter Payton Man of the Year in the NFL. We actually called a simple play: all go routes, aka menu nine, the perfect plan for the way the Bulldogs were positioned.

Thomas was matched up right over the top of me, so, on the snap of the ball, I gave him a swim move at the line of scrimmage. Just as I did that to create the slightest bit of separation, Rex threw the football up almost like an alley-oop in basketball. He knew, given the motion and movements of our bodies, that Thomas wouldn't have enough time to react if the ball was placed perfectly. And it was. Rex trusted his instincts and I merely did what I was asked to do. It was honestly Rex who did the hard part.

It's amazing that something that happened so fast, literally in an instant, was so simple and so complex at the same time and also came with such a lasting legacy. As I am still either celebrated or chastised for, depending on where I am, the magnitude of that play was far greater than it just being one more big win for Florida. Georgia entered that Saturday ranked fifth nationally. Mark Richt's Bulldogs went on to have one of their best seasons in program history, going 13-1 and finishing third in the final AP poll. As that record clearly indicates, Georgia ended the year with just one loss. I, along with Rex Grossman and so many others, had a little bit to do with that.

If you want to let the mind wander, play what-if games and have a little fun at a rival's expense, an argument can be made that my touchdown catch may have kept the Bulldogs from winning a national championship.

Now there is no guarantee that Georgia would have beaten Miami or Ohio State. I'm just glad the Bulldogs didn't get the chance.

Depending on where I am in the Deep South, some people tell me how much they love me; others, slightly to the north, not so much. That border is more than just a state line, it's a line of scrimmage.

Thinking back to 1980, consider Rex Grossman-to-Ben Troupe the reverse Buck Belue-to-Lindsay Scott. It was revenge a lifetime later.

Here is the thing about the Georgia Bulldogs, coming from a Georgia boy. Like any fan who bleeds orange and blue, I hate them and I hate everything about them. I can even name a few reasons why for specific clarification: the Bulldogs rarely win the big game, they are always overrated and overhyped, every recruiting class is their best ever, their logo and uniforms are a less colorful version of the Green Bay Packers, their fans literally bark in public and, I'll say it, I don't even like the little dog. Smokey, from Tennessee, is way more fun and I don't really like him either.

With all of that said, Florida wouldn't be Florida without Georgia. Our stories are constantly intertwined and I appreciate and respect that. Though I have a significant disdain for who we play down there, I love Jacksonville and love the setting that comes with it. Florida needs Georgia and Georgia needs Florida. If you don't have someone to measure your success against, you really never know how good you are. Without our archrival, the last Saturday in October is just another Saturday in October. We have plenty of Saturdays. Our day deserves to stand out and stand alone.

Admittedly, the Bulldogs do have an impressive resume all their own. I may not have liked guys like David Greene and David Pollack, Thomas Davis or Terrance Edwards, but I always respected them. I needed them. Throughout my post-football media career, some of my favorite interviews have come by way of talking to former Georgia stars such as Gerald Anderson, John Lastinger, Josh Mallard and Richard Samuel, greats who attended my inaugural Florida-Georgia Legends Series on Jekyll Island in 2019 the night before the big game. I've always cherished my conversations with D.J. Shockley, Russ Tanner and Tim Worley.

Furthermore, I've been wowed by the perspective of long-time Georgia journalist Murray Poole, who covered over 50 straight Florida-Georgia games during his esteemed writing career.

Swainsboro is and always will be a Bulldog town. It goes without saying that tracks of red clay marked my move to Gainesville. From Swainsboro to Augusta to Atlanta to Georgia's coast, much of my adult life has been spent living in the Peach State, a fact I'm quick and proud to admit. Though I've worn the numbers 84 and 86, I represent the 478, the 706 and the 912. Georgia is in my heart and in my soul.

My weekends ease their way on like a Ray Charles song. People talk about the big cities and beaches of Florida, the Panhandle, the Muck or the Everglades. I love Georgia's dirty ocean water, our sticky heat, the foothills of what I call mountains, the towns with one stop-light and the old country squares where they rest. I love the independence of Savannah, the backroads to Macon and the beautiful diversity of Atlanta. I see myself in the people of all of those places.

I've been fortunate enough to travel and live all over the United States and experience the great people and wonderful cultures in amazing places like New York City and the Bay Area. Those tabs on my timeline helped me understand just how small we all are.

That said, I need my Sundays with a service and my iced tea real sweet. Quite literally, you will only see me wearing hats with an "A" on them and that letter that doesn't stand for "anywhere". Long live Atlanta. Long live Georgia. I will gladly drink the leftover juice from a Vienna Sausage can, a delicacy where I'm from. I still get in my car at night just to ride around. I'm more Bankhead than Buckhead, but I'm Georgia through and through. I'm still in awe of the fact that I actually turned the Bulldogs down.

Monday through Friday, I run Georgia like a route tree. Every Saturday in the fall, however, my leaves lay on more hallowed turf.

In 2016, I was stunned and thrilled to be inducted into the famed Florida-Georgia Hall of Fame. My class was star-studded, featuring former Florida kicker Jeff Chandler, along with former Georgia defensive lineman Marcus Stroud, former safety Scott Woerner and beloved CBS Sports broadcaster Verne Lundquist. It was my complete and utter privilege to be recognized amongst those gentlemen and to be honored at a banquet that featured many standouts from, in my opinion, the greatest rivalry in all of college football.

I visited with so many at an elegant banquet held at the home of the Jaguars in Jacksonville as we were enshrined. From fans sharing their memories of our big moments to former players reflecting on their own glory days, the afternoon became one big highlight reel.

Though my eyes remained fixed on every presentation, then on those in attendance as I gave my speech, my heart never left our table. There sat my parents, the two people most responsible for all that I was getting to experience. I was in the spotlight, but they were worthy of that glow. My hope is that when they saw the bust of my college-aged self, they both saw themselves in it as well. It was their work that was really on display.

There was a special magic to that moment, so much so that my infant niece Jamie, barely old enough to open her eyes, calmly rested through the entire banquet, gently grinning and never making a sound. With so many instances that stood out, the one that mattered the most to me, while sitting next to former Florida Athletic Director Jeremy Foley on the big stage, was being able to wave at and make faces with my daughter Yaya in the crowd. I couldn't stop smiling.

Along with even more members of my family, we were all recognized on the field, standing next to the likes of Tim Tebow, the very next day. That was the first Florida game I had been to since the end of my playing career. And it was a good one, with the good guys winning. Throughout the entire afternoon, a dozen Troupes from map dots in the heart of Georgia stayed Florida loud and proud. Lucus joined me on the field for my official recognition, which meant a lot to me given where he was and what he was doing back when I was playing.

My children, dressed in their bright orange and blue, were introduced to the art of trash-talking. They know that daddy went 4-0 in the series and will be quick to tell you about it, too. Yaya, my nephew Rian and niece Jalin were even on the jumbotron and got the crowd cheering when they started dancing on the big screen.

For a boy from a small town in the state, I will always pay special attention to what Georgia is doing. And if they ever win another national championship, I might have to move. I can't take more from the worst fan base in the country than I already do and have to. Understand, though, that Georgia is part of my Florida story and not just because of what happened on that fateful third-and-goal. We keep our friends close, but our enemies closer.

As any map will tell you, Florida and Georgia are packed tight like hot dogs in a package. Camden and Nassau counties stand a stone's throw apart on I-95. That said, they are a world away each season.

All that I was able to accomplish at Florida, the Georgia play included, was a team-wide achievement. For me, coming to Gainesville as part of the heralded class of 2000, I always felt a special bond with those guys in particular. We won together, we lost together and, quite frankly, we figured it all out together. On the field and off. I will always be tied to Cory Bailey, Brock Berlin, Jonathan Colon, Ronald Dowdy, Dewayne DuBose, Reid Fleming, Willie Green, Travis Harris, Kelvin Kight, Matt Jackson, Darrell Lee, Bennie Mills, Kenny Parker, Carlos

Perez, Thomas Pittman, Keiwan Ratliff, Gus Scott, Ian Scott, O.J. Small, Earnest Smith, Shannon Snell, Max Starks, Chad Tidwell (even though he was from Tallahassee) and Bobby Williams.

Some of them remain close friends of mine to this day. I think about every single one of them often as they all helped mold me into the man I am now.

There wasn't the widespread coverage of recruiting that there currently is, but I did know about Brock Berlin as he was ranked by many as the number one player in the country coming out of high school. We actually played against him after he transferred to Miami. I remember meeting Max Starks, who stood 6'8'' and spoke like a British aristocrat. With me being from the country part of the country, I was thinking, "...who in the world is this dude?" His real name, by the way, is Maximillian Weisner Starks IV; put some respect on the official title of the two-time Super Bowl champion.

I went on my recruiting visit to Florida with Ronald Dowdy. I learned all about Darrell Lee's background, coming in from Missouri. Carlos Perez was the first Dominican man I ever met and the first black person who spoke Spanish. I became an extended part of Gus Scott's family.

The biggest difference in high school and college for us was that everything had a purpose. There was no wasted time, no wasted movement. Practice was direct, fast and organized. Potentially playing in an actual game didn't even dawn on me my first few months in Gainesville as I was just trying to get the whole routine down. You know, remember where to go and when to be there.

A lot of people don't realize how overwhelming the life of a student-athlete can be. About 99% of the time, it's not glamorous. A lot of the time it isn't even fun. Most of the time, you aren't even aware of all that is going on around you, much less a part of it. That was especially the case for me as, with my mother's signature, I actually enrolled at Florida at only 17 years old. I was baby-faced and my mind wasn't all that far ahead.

I was surprised at how many others actually knew who I was. Uncomfortable with it, even. People knew more about me than *me*; my football statistics, my recruiting rankings, where I might fit in on the depth chart, how much I weighed, how much I lifted and what I had better be doing if I wanted to see the field. Like everybody else, I was scared, homesick and uneasy about this whole transition that I had worked so hard to be able to make.

I thought about transferring myself, constantly wondering if I should leave and what might happen if I did. Trying to manage my schoolwork, my team obligations and my own emotional growth, I even wondered if football was really right for me or if Florida was the place where I truly fit in. The answer was obviously yes, but it took a lot of people to help me finally see it all so clearly.

I committed to and signed with the legendary Steve Spurrier. When he walked into my living room and asked, "Bennie," as he calls me, "are you with us?", my only reaction was to smile and say yes. His simple-but-strong conviction as one of the greats of the game was more than enough for me. Though I didn't know everything about him, as I was still learning about the history and tradition of college football, my cousin Purcell told me that you never tell Steve Spurrier no. That and Mama constantly prayed about the decision and kept seeing gators in her dreams.

Coach Spurrier was just different than all of the other coaches. He carried himself in a way that projected a crisp and clean arrogance. One you had to respect. Compared to the other men who recruited me, like Georgia's Jim Donnan, Coach Spurrier stood out. On my visit to Georgia, Coach Donnan, who was a nice guy, welcomed me into his office while eating a chili dog with stains on his shirt. For some reason, those things mattered to me as a strangely-observant teenager.

The energy around Coach Spurrier was different than the other coaches I met, though the interest from all of them was humbling. I once had Tommy Bowden, Lou Holtz and Coach Donnan in the principal's office at Butler High School. When Coach Holtz visited my house, Coach Bowden was in the parking lot waiting outside. One left and another came in. These faces were all part of the recruiting process.

In Coach Spurrier, I saw a man who knew what he was doing. I also saw a rock star, an offensive genius and a winner. I saw the swagger.

While Coach Spurrier may have been one of the main reasons I became a Gator, my interactions with him on campus were actually fairly limited. A lot of fans might be surprised by this, but regular players don't spend a lot of time with the head coach. Especially as underclassmen. They are so busy, with so many different roles to play, that they are basically heads-of-state with a number of assistants who work directly with the team. Any football program comes with a large and complex group of staff members, helpers who go well beyond just the assistant coaches on the sidelines. That infrastructure was critically important for me.

I immediately learned the basics from Rob Glass, who was Florida's outstanding strength and conditioning coach. There is no chance I would have made it without him. People just don't know how much strength coaches do for a football team. While the NCAA has limits on when and how often on-field coaches can work with players, the strength staff serves as their fill-in. Their roles go well beyond the critical work they do of readying our bodies for the season to come.

Strength coaches are part teacher, part guidance counselor, part psychologist and, honestly, part parent for so many young men. Before I could walk, much less run, Coach Glass helped me find my footing on campus. He and Tyke Tolbert, my position coach, taught me how to prepare myself, then how to believe in myself. For all of the measurables, those are the traits that make the most difference. They both got the best out of me.

Coach Tolbert was instrumental in me making it to the next level. It's worth saying again and again; there is simply no way I would have had the career I did without him and Coach Glass. I also benefited greatly from being around our defensive coordinator Charlie Strong, a great role model and a great leader. His nickname was "Tubb", a fact I learned while sharing a special Thanksgiving dinner at his home. Legendary receiver coach Dwayne Dixon also made a big impact on me as I worked with him my senior year.

Those I learned from at Florida didn't always have direct roles on the football team. Dr. Keith Carodine, who helped all of us players become better student-athletes and people, was a professor, an advisor and a mentor. He was always reminding us of the big picture. People in sports information like Steve McClain and Mike Spiegler helped ready us for our introduction to the media, also making sure that our stories were told as we grew as Gators. There was Alecia in public relations, Ashley Bowman Brouillette in compliance, William "Pizza Bill" Feinberg and Tim Sain in equipment and trainer Chris Patrick, among others.

It's worth sharing that I also learned a lot from players on Florida's other athletic teams. I had many close friends who played women's basketball, including Vanessa Hayden, who became one of the standout performers in SEC history and the 7th overall pick in the 2004 WNBA Draft. She used to wear overalls, a style that resembled my own country flow. Our collective struggles were often as relatable as our individual stories. Even with all that was going on with our respective schedules, sometimes it was good to just talk.

Of all of the people that I have ever met, boy could Coach Spurrier talk. Tone rising as his did, his phrases sometimes came out weird and he often stopped midway like he was muttering or whispering under his breath. Those tirades were, yes, sometimes accompanied by his famed visor throw, which he did actually do. Coach Spurrier, though, had swagger before it was in style. It wasn't exaggerated, either. What you saw was who he is.

Think about this man, born in, of all places, Miami Beach. I always get asked how Coach Spurrier was. My answer will always be that he was authentic, the same in public and in private. He was also genuine. He took the time to know more about his players than what was merely in the media guide. What people will never appreciate is that Coach Spurrier wanted to know me as more than just a football player. He wanted to know more about all of us.

One time on my recruiting visit, Coach Spurrier took me into his trophy room in his home. I actually saw his Heisman Trophy and tried to touch it. Right before I did, with it feeling like my hand was moving in slow motion, he suddenly told us all to leave. But I did get to go into his house, which was quite meaningful. Coach Spurrier's place was actually pretty modest. That made sense because Coach Spurrier is both big-time and down to earth. He is a cool cat. Through that, Coach Spurrier let me know that life will always be both perception and reality.

Coach Spurrier won a Heisman Trophy as a player, changed the way football was played as a head coach and won his national championship over our in-state rival Florida State and did so by a score of 52-21. Coach Spurrier was affably smug and bold and, because of that, he never needed to come up with a dramatic motivational speech or work hard to set the scene. His conviction and simple belief that he and we were the best was the unrelenting expectation for all of us. It was empowering.

While some people may be confident, Coach Spurrier was convinced. He played to win and, much to the chagrin of his opponents, did so regardless of the score. It simply wasn't in Coach Spurrier to not try to put up points or, at a bare minimum, not use the precious game repetitions he valued so much to prepare younger or less experienced players for what was potentially one day to come. Coach Spurrier always kept coming, until there was no time left on the clock.

As most geniuses are, Coach Spurrier was often off in his own world. Somewhere in there he was a pigskin pioneer, drawing up plays that would change the way offenses would be utilized forever. Even years after his retirement, schemes you see now still have Coach Spurrier's fingerprints all over them. He was also always working on his tan and perfecting his golf game.

Take out the fact that Coach Spurrier is one of the greatest players to ever play at Florida, he simply had to coach the Gators. With all due respect to Duke, South Carolina and his stint with Washington in the NFL, those fits really weren't ever right. While at the helm of one of the biggest jobs in the sport, Coach Spurrier was an extension of everything Ocala. He will always be standing on the fairway somewhere, shaggy hair tucked under an orange and blue visor, complaining about the clouds and wondering what's for lunch. Beyond just representing Florida, Coach Spurrier is Florida. So is his wife Jerri and his assistant Jamie.

If "We are the boys from old Florida", Coach Spurrier was, is and forever will be, the man.

Now that doesn't mean everything he did was cool. On the bus ride to Doak Campbell Stadium to play Florida State my freshman year, Coach Spurrier stood up to share some comments on the game. He then said that he wanted to play us a song, which was kind of odd and out of place. It only got weirder from there. He played a dreary, depressing, slow country tune called "I Hope You Dance" by Lee Ann Womack.

Too scared to say anything but absolutely incapable of dancing or singing along, we all looked around at each other without any mood changes or facial expressions. None of us knew what to do. None of us knew what to say. A strange, tense silence, aside from that constant wailing, came over the bus. Coach Spurrier, of course, didn't pick up on any of it and thought his choice of hit was the perfect gameday starter. That Steve Spurrer was his Johnson City, Tennessee side.

While Steve Spurrier was the coach I chose to play for, Ron Zook was the coach I needed. Florida's next head coaching hire when Spurrier left for the NFL, Coach Zook's arrival coincided with my rise. Regarding that coaching change, I always laugh when there is an assumption that players have inside knowledge regarding a situation like that. I found out Coach Spurrier was leaving while driving back home from the Orange Bowl with Kenny Parker.

Interestingly enough, Coach Spurrier had just finished telling us returning players how we would be moving into leadership roles on the team. I supported him chasing his opportunities at the next level, mind you. Coach Spurrier had accomplished everything there was to accomplish in college football and he needed to make the most of his chance to get that NFL money. As players, we were all hoping to do the same one day.

When it comes to coaches, there is no loyalty in sports and everybody, regardless of what your contract says, is one or two bad seasons away from getting fired. It has to go both ways. With Coach Spurrier moving towards the latter part of his career, I certainly could not fault him for taking one of the 32 head coaching jobs at football's highest level. Especially after 12 iconic seasons as the head coach at Florida, 17 total years if you count his award-winning playing career and one season as an assistant. Coach Spurrier did his thing and I can respect that. We all know where his heart is.

What Coach Zook did was come in and challenge me, directly and indirectly alike. I'll be honest, I didn't like him at all when he first came to Gainesville. He was unapologetically blunt, to the point and bottom-line based. Coach Zook came to Florida from the NFL as he was previously the defensive coordinator for the New Orleans Saints. He was no-nonsense and demanded a constant attention to detail. That was a bit of a change from Coach Spurrier, who was more of a "player's coach" and obviously had a track record in town and around the country that spoke for itself.

Coach Zook was a midwestern guy, from Ohio. Though he had been at Florida as an assistant, he was a different cultural fit than the legend he was replacing. To come right in after Coach Spurrier, you had to be a little bit crazy and have a strong mindset to handle the unrealistic expectations that were obviously still in place.

We went 8-5 Coach Zook's first year, played a half-dozen nationally-ranked teams, beat number four Tennessee and number five Georgia and the reaction was that we just had the worst season in school history. We played seven ranked opponents in 2003, won at number six LSU and number eleven Arkansas and beat UGA, ranked number four, in Jacksonville again and the feedback was more of the same. Such is life at Florida, which Coach Zook and we all understood.

Prior to that game in Baton Rouge, with us at 3-3 overall, Gator great Willie Jackson told me that if we lost to the Tigers and had a losing record, we shouldn't even get back on the plane.

Interestingly enough, Coach Zook's last game with the Gators was a 20-13 victory over Florida State in Tallahassee, On the day the Seminoles dedicated their field to the great Bobby Bowden, it was Coach Zook who was carried off of it in victory.

Early in his tenure, Coach Zook made an impact on me. He flat out told me that the way I practiced simply wasn't good enough. I felt disrespected, but he was right. I was cheating the system and not making the most of my opportunities. That applied in more ways than one. Coach Zook helped me understand the big picture. As was often the case with he and I, it took me some time to fully appreciate all that he was saying. But Coach Zook was always right.

One night, me and some teammates were out at a club and the drinks started flowing. Then the melee started. Then the cops came. Though I wasn't drinking or fighting, I was there as some of my teammates were and got arrested for it. Coach Zook called me into his office the very next day. To my initial surprise, he sternly, almost-tearfully, told me that I had failed my teammates. Coach

Zook told me that I let all of that happen and that I was responsible for them getting locked up. When I started to explain myself, he blurted out for me to stop and strongly explained to me, once again, that I let all of this happen. I certainly didn't stop it.

Right then and there, Coach Zook told me that I was his best player, but that I would not be treated like it. He helped me realize that while I was on a team, I was not yet part of a team. I had not earned that. When I sheepishly responded by saying that I was just one person who couldn't affect everyone else, he promptly corrected me by telling me that Martin Luther King, Jr. held the March on Washington long before there was even any way to communicate with the public at large. He demanded that I understand that one person gave one speech on one day and changed the world. Leaders must be responsible for everyone.

One of my other early experiences with Coach Zook was a shock, one that embarrassed me but also made me a better player and teammate all at once. I went into his office one day and told him that I wanted to talk. I was unhappy with my spot on the depth chart, felt I deserved more playing time and felt, selfishly, that I was a better player than the guys in front of me. In what I thought was a private discussion, he listened and seemed receptive. I didn't know just how much attention he was paying to everything I said.

Later that week before practice, Coach Zook was addressing the team and his words and glare turned to me. He called on me directly, singled me out in front of everyone and suggested that I had something that I wanted to say to the whole team. Newsflash, I didn't. I acted aloof and tried to play off what a man I didn't quite understand yet was wanting me to do. Coach Zook and the rest of the room all perked up and awaited my response. I was ready in private, but not in public. Coach Zook was teaching me a lesson and was doing so by letting my silence speak for itself.

I didn't know what to say, but, moving forward, I did know how to act. I learned, the hard way, that complaining privately isn't more important than performing publicly. In my mind, I thought I was something because Coach Spurrier recruited me. Coach Zook was showing me the wrong way and the right way of going about things. When he gave me the platform I asked for, I froze. In those moments, Coach Zook was showing me who I was when I came into his office. He was summarizing my entire attitude with one situation.

In that moment, that shame helped me. My selfishness was on full display. What happened opened my eyes to the work that everyone else was doing, helped bring my flaws to the forefront and helped reinforce the idea that we were all striving towards the same goals. I was good, but I wasn't unique. If I wanted more playing time, I had to earn it.

Coach Zook utilized the tight end more consistently than Coach Spurrier and that obviously helped elevate my profile. He benefited me in ways that went beyond my responsibilities on the field, however. Coach Zook never once let me settle. Like a tube of toothpaste, he squeezed every ounce of talent out of me. From early on, Coach Zook trained me to be an every down tight end and helped me recognize that everything I did, from leading the way at practice to understanding the full offensive playbook, was related to that.

There were times where I hated Coach Zook, wanted to fight him even, but tough love is sometimes the love you need. It's hard to grow when you are comfortable, at least that was the case for me. Beyond those difficult lessons, Coach Zook was well-versed in what it took to be successful in the NFL and well-connected from his time spent in the league. Before my pro day or the NFL Combine, Coach Zook prepared me to make the most of those opportunities.

If Steve Spurrier and Jeff Fisher were the two slices of bread on my football sandwich, Ron Zook was the meat in the middle. Coach Zook used to tell my mama to tell me to not forget about him. *Don't worry Coach, I never will.* His impact on me remains.

Through initial disappointments and coaching changes, I finally started to find my way at Florida. After only one catch my freshman year and nine as a sophomore, I caught 15 passes as a junior, but I also started to feel more comfortable and get noticed. Following our Outback Bowl loss to Michigan, where I had a nice 27-yard catch, a reporter came up to me, a tight end with 25 career receptions, and asked if I was going pro. Yet again, I didn't know what to say.

The NFL had never really crossed my mind. As multiple teammates would soon explain to me, though, that is how the hype machine works. As a junior, boosted by my performance in the Georgia game, there was an outside expectation that I had the chance to be moving into a more prominent position. With that naturally came another progression: my name became a more common one and my face a more recognizable one.

From media to fans, people started talking about my future. Even if it didn't make sense, the anticipation that I might be becoming someone came with questions that I had never even considered. The next few months would come with even more.

Before I was ever even a consistent part of our offensive production, my veteran familiarity came with a spotlight. People started approaching me. I started doing interviews on a regular basis. I was even used for some Florida football promotional material. Other players would come up to me and say, "you're the one now."

There was one occurrence, in particular, that stopped me in my tracks. On a regular trip to Publix to buy Swiss Rolls, I was walking through the aisles and I saw, among the faces of celebrities and politicians, me. I, Ben Troupe, with only a handful of games on my resume with more than one catch, was on the cover of a national college football magazine. I was suddenly on a store bookshelf.

A lot of emotions came with that. First and foremost, I couldn't buy many copies of any magazine as such spending simply wasn't in my budget. My daddy literally dropped me off at Florida as a freshman with a 20-dollar bill. I was broke. It's a strange realization to see something with you on it, yet not really be able to afford it, much less get paid because of it.

Secondarily, I was still introducing myself to classmates on the first day of each semester, now I was in stores all across the southeast? Seeing myself on the cover of a magazine was exciting, but also confusing. Did I have to play better now? How would my teammates feel? Was I wrong for wanting compensation for something like this? What would my family and friends back home think?

Each glance was humbling, though I didn't feel like I deserved the product placement. Later, every store or gas station I went into had Florida's number 84 on the cover. I couldn't decide if that was really me or someone else.

The persona of what people expect you to be when you are an athlete is one I still struggle with. You almost have to be that other person more than the person you really are. It's a transformation that started at Florida for me. Thousands of people, maybe even millions, knew who I was. They knew my name and number, but they didn't know me. "Ben" may have been a star, but "Benjamin" was often confused and uncertain of how to respond to it all. I have never been a social person.

It was as if my own shadow was following me everywhere I went, with the real me actually being the reflection.

So much of what I experienced at Florida was surreal; Coach Spurrier's resignation, the SEC Championship Game, the Orange Bowl, the Georgia play, my last home game against Florida State. Those who followed our team had no idea what it was like to spend so much time with the guys. Many memories are cherished ones I will always reflect on.

Some were horrible moments that I will never forget. My sophomore year, we had a freshman fullback named Eraste Autin who suffered heat stroke at practice and died six days later. That news was unthinkable, an event nobody knew how to deal with. Though we played the entire season with his name sewn on our jerseys, a lot of us never got the chance to get to really know him. It was a terrible tragedy. As a team, we struggled to process it.

I remember talking with a campus police officer who told me that, while he had seen a lot during his career, he had never seen anything like what happened to Eraste. That officer explained to me how deeply struck he was by it all. So many were. May Eraste rest in peace.

A football team is a special thing and a locker room is a special place. The bond we all shared with each other was incredible and, though imperfect, it was real. In our locker room, we had superstars in the offensive backfield like Rex Grossman and Chris Leak, Ciatrick Fason and Earnest Graham. We had straight-up ballers representing "DBU" like Keiwan Ratliff and Lito Sheppard. Rex, obviously, should have won the Heisman Trophy in 2001. Maybe if I would have actually done a little more to help him, he would have.

Nobody on our team, not all of us combined, would become the celebrity that Thaddeus Bullard would. Thad, who almost always had his shirt off, was a bald body-builder in orange and blue. He was a physical specimen and had all of those muscles around your belly that make your torso look so good. Now either he had perfected the art of timely sweating or he secretly oiled himself up, but Thad was always glistening and shining in the sun. He was a showman.

On the field, and I mean this with all due respect, I honestly don't remember anything about him. Admittedly, some of my memories from practices and even some from games have started to fade, but I can't think of a single instance where Thad was actually out there.

A lot more engaged and involved around campus than the rest of us, Thad always had something to do, somewhere to be. He wouldn't attend some practices or team events and apparently he got permission to miss from the coaches because of everything else he did away from football. Thad was smart. He was a networker and a go-getter. You know those student clubs where they will offer you free pizza just to attend? Thad wasn't just at those, he was hosting them. Being a student-athlete really is two full-time jobs; somehow, Thad found time for three.

He helped organize meetings and set up events, just for starters. Thad became connected with multiple groups at Florida, the football team being merely one of them. Even then, he was kind of a big deal. One weekend, the great Snoop Dogg had a concert on campus. Daryl Lee, Ronald Dowdy and I went to the show. I wore a pair of all-white patent-leather Jordans, my first Js ever. I thought I was something else. When I finally got close enough to see Snoop, he was really into the atmosphere and interacting with the crowd.

In addition to hyping up us Gators on stage, Snoop actually had on a real Florida football jersey. As I got close enough to see, I noticed it was Thaddeus Bullard's.

While most probably don't know Thad, millions around the world know Titus O'Neil. Thad, under his ring name, has gone on to become one of the most famous and popular wrestlers in the WWE. Fans know Thad as Titus, but we used to call him "T-Bull". Along with everything else he was doing at the time, Thad was carving out the start of his career.

"Gator Nation" should be very proud of Thad, just as I am. Not only because of his professional accomplishments, but because of his personal ones. Thad's charity work, particularly in the Tampa area, has helped and inspired countless people. He has worked tirelessly to improve less-fortunate neighborhoods, focusing on safety and accessible outside opportunities. He has led reading initiatives, healthy eating campaigns and toy drives for underprivileged and sick youth. Thad has been honored with a number of community awards and civic distinctions. Big muscles and body slams aside, he is a great person and deserves to be recognized for that.

Titus O'Neil is just one example of the many personalities we had on our teams. I certainly understand that football, if we are being completely honest, is why many of us were at Florida. That said, I am so grateful that I was able to see so many of the people behind the players.

Football is a unique sport because the equipment makes us look bigger than we actually are. It also prevents fans, especially with college football, from seeing how young we truly are. The context of the game almost presents us all as mighty gladiators, warriors impervious to weakness, clashing each week in some grand arena.

To paraphrase LeBron James here, we are all more than just athletes. Sports, even if it seems like it is, isn't all we do.

Beyond just Thad, dozens of my former teammates have gone on to become doctors, lawyers, civil servants, educators, medical professionals, financial experts, media members, advocates, volunteers, husbands and fathers. The stories you don't see are even more important than the ones that you do.

My Florida family was and remains a big one. I continue to be amazed at the post-football work so many of these men are doing. Our time as Gators never really ended, our uniforms just changed. All that we learned at Florida, going well beyond the football field, was preparing us for life and, in reality, that only meant the NFL for a select few of us. Even for those of us fortunate to play professional football, that only delayed our inevitable transition back into the real world. Florida definitely helped prepare us for that, even when we weren't paying full attention. I become more and more appreciative of my time in Gainesville the longer I am away from it.

Others will always recall the games we played. I certainly will, too. Beating LSU in Death Valley was a once-in-a-lifetime experience. So was winning the Orange Bowl, playing in the Sugar Bowl and all of the pageantry that comes with the postseason.

It simply does not get much bigger than claiming an SEC Championship. If I'm being truthful, I probably didn't have much to do with that. I was front and center in that postgame photo, though! There is nothing in the sport like the environment down in Jacksonville, a statement that is even more true, look up those results from 2000-2003, when you win every year. Going up against tradition rich programs like Auburn, Florida State, Miami, Michigan and Tennessee helped me better understand the history of the game I was playing.

The trips themselves are something special. Before signing with Florida, I had only been out of the state of Georgia a handful of times. With how I saw the south, I basically saw the world.

Beyond playing in front of the best fans in the loudest stadium in the country every home Saturday, I got to see 100,000 people in orange in Knoxville and 100,000 more in purple and gold in Baton Rouge. I played against Eli Manning in the Grove in Oxford, saw the eagle fly around Jordan-Hare Stadium at Auburn and Chief Osceola plant the spear in Tallahassee. I faced the Hurricanes when "The U" was "The U". I did so in New Orleans, our pre-game throwdown on Bourbon Street included, at home and in the old Orange Bowl, the O.G. Orange Bowl.

I didn't know much about college football before I signed my scholarship, but I fell in love with it not long after. Years after jumping over defenders, I remain head over heels.

I'm glad to talk about all of those moments and to share how incredible they were. When I give speeches or do interviews now, fans often ask me about the best atmosphere or the best venue I ever played in. Those are hard questions to answer. Each home stadium in the SEC is a buffet of chaos and crazy. LSU definitely stood out.

Every place has its own sights and sounds, but, know this, my favorite game day experience will never change. And I don't even have to say what it was, is and forever will be. The Swamp is that deal. Instead of offering my two cents on the subject, I will just offer my *Two Bits*, instead.

What college football really turns out to be is what happens away from the bright lights and the big stage. I left campus with All-American and All-SEC plaques, SEC and Orange Bowl Championship rings and on-field memories that will last me a lifetime. I should have also left with a couch.

In the little free time that I had at Florida, I would often poke around the facility as I was, even as a player, just fascinated by all that was going on. A couple of times a week, I would head upstairs and chat with some of the compliance and sports information people like Mike Speigler. It was really interesting to see all that they did and that is how I developed relationships with other folks around the program. These individuals weren't coaches, but they were very important to the daily functioning of all of the sports teams. They also did a whole lot of work.

One of the assistants there, a guy by the name of Jamie McClouskey, had an office with a couch in it. I became friends with him and we talked a few times each week. It got to the point where I would regularly come into Jamie's office and lay down on that couch. You know, like patients do with psychologists, I guess. These visits with Jamie, and that couch, became a normal part of my routine. In some ways, that couch meant more to me than any trophy or piece of memorabilia I received. I grew up there. I learned about everything that I was doing there.

Years after I left campus, I heard from old friends that Jamie, for some reason, had desperately tried to contact me while I was in the NFL. At first, I wondered why. Then, it made sense. More than just that, it made me appreciate all of the people who were always there for me.

They said Jamie took another job and upon cleaning out his office in Gainesville, he literally wanted me to have that old couch and was willing to box and ship it to me on his dime to get it to me in Nashville. I had a new phone number, probably wasn't as generally accessible as I should have been and we never actually got in touch.

But that, when I talk about what college football really is, is what college football really is. It's the people, the places and the things along the way.

THE CREW

As you hear a lot, a football team really is a family. Even within a family, though, especially an extended one with over 100 people, you have those you spend more time with than others. One of the great misconceptions about sports in my mind is that most fans think we all are best friends who leave practice or a game and all go chill at the same house or restaurant, bar or club. That is simply not the case. That doesn't mean I didn't support, care for or work right alongside all of my teammates at Florida, I just didn't personally know them the way some might have thought I did. Given the numbers and all of our busy schedules, it wasn't even possible.

I often thought about whether or not all of our coaches even distinctly knew everybody on the roster. The short answer is probably not, though I have to give Coach Spurrier credit as every time I see him, and I was not a standout on his teams, he comes up to me and says, "hey, Bennie". I am always impressed by that.

A college football team is big, with people coming together from all over the country and with a lot of moving parts. A football facility can become a fluid mass of humanity. There is so much going on, it's hard to keep up.

Two examples of this would be my relationship with my star quarterbacks, perhaps the most recognizable players on any of our teams in Rex Grossman and Chris Leak. Rex would go on to compete in Super Bowl XLI. With our famous play in Jacksonville, people have approached me talking about Rex, especially, as if we spent large parts of the day together for years. They always expect me to go full Terrell Owens on it and cry out, "that's my quarterback!"

I am forever grateful that I was able to play with such an outstanding signal caller. Obviously, Rex and I interacted directly in practice and in games. He, as my career started to peak, was largely responsible for that progression. Rex was stunningly accurate, was a great dude and he truly is a Gator legend. I still can't believe he lost the 2001 Heisman Trophy to Nebraska's Eric Crouch.

When Rex and I were playing, however, I didn't even know where he lived, much less what he did. I never once saw Rex outside of football. He and I didn't go to the same places or do the same things. If I'm remembering correctly, I think some of my friends did take me by his place right after he declared for the NFL Draft. Apparently he had an old TV that he was giving away, so we found our way over to vie for the prize. I really didn't know that much about Rex, except that he could throw that football.

I never spent time with Chris Leak away from the football field, either. A lot of that was because of our ages. I was a senior, when Chris was a freshman. Though he was my quarterback during my best season, we, like many teammates in different classes, just didn't know each other away from the game. That said, I did try my best to be a mentor for him and help take away some of the immense pressure he was facing as a very young player. Chris delivered such a pretty pass. Like Rex, he made it easy for me. It was beautiful to watch Chris throw the football. He helped me make it to the NFL.

Rex was the best quarterback I played with at Florida, but Chris was built to play the quarterback position. I just didn't know either of them personally.

That was the case with a lot of my teammates. Of course, I felt a bond with them as I shared many of the same goals they had and we shared a lot of the same experiences. That said, when people asked me what Rex was like around campus, and this happened more and more as he became a leading Heisman Trophy candidate, my answer was always the same: I really didn't know. Same with Chris. Same with a lot of guys.

As it is with any large group of people, various factors resulted in smaller groups of friends emerging. I was a sociology major and, given that I tried my best in school, I should be able to explain some of this. Let's get the obvious and uncomfortable, at least for some, out of the way; honestly, most of the black guys stayed around black guys and most of the white guys stayed around white guys. This wasn't due to some level of uncomfortability, it was just a natural byproduct of the situation. It was simple. We were coming from different backgrounds and quickly gathering together in a new, foreign place.

Young and largely inexperienced when it came to anything resembling adult life, we gravitated towards people that had similar stories to us, liked the same things as us and, to be blunt, looked like us. There wasn't any intentional separation and we all got along as teammates. Just like in high school, however, there were various cliques of people on the squad.

Some of this, remember, simply came down to time. With our schedules, there weren't enough hours in the day for us to meet and greet all of our teammates and spend time with them away from the field. Just like I wasn't necessarily personally close with Rex Grossman or Chris Leak, the same can be said for Thaddeus Bullard, Jeff Chandler, Channing Crowder, Taylor Jacobs, Shannon Snell and many of the other players, even well-known stars like those referenced. I didn't personally know all of the coaches, either.

When fans are surprised when they hear that a college football team isn't always a clubhouse full of best friends or that we never had a yearbook we all signed and voted on different distinctions for, I always ask if they spend time after hours with everyone they work with? It has always been interesting to me that people are so surprised by this. It was even more true in the NFL.

My crew was me, Guss Scott, Darrell Lee, Ronald Dowdy and Carlos Perez, the "Fab Five". We all came in together as part of the class of 2000, which is a key marker of who players align themselves with. You are always closer with your classmates.

As incoming freshmen, we just didn't know much about all of the upperclassmen. We, with a few exceptions, didn't hang out together outside of football, either. Early in my career, the "'97 Boys" were the big men on campus. Veterans like Alex Brown, Andra Davis, Buck Gurley, Thomas Moody and Gerard Warren formed a different group than ours. Most incoming classes were that way. And there was nothing wrong with that. Outside of merely what we did for fun, each inner-circle lived in different places, had other buildings we went to for classes and separate responsibilities.

There are just so many people on a football team and within a football program. I don't want to create the perception that our locker room was divided as it never was. Our team chemistry was actually always great and so was our communication. I do, however, want there to be a better outside understanding of how most large locker room environments really are. This was all part of my adjustment.

What made my tight group so unique, and what allowed all of us to be ourselves, is how different we all were. There was a lot of personality on our teams at Florida and my crew was no different. That encouraged our own individuality to continue to grow. For me, this was the first time I got introduced to real friendship. In Swainsboro, I always viewed people like Titus Peeples as a brother with a different last name. I made my first friends in Gainesville.

Guss Scott, the best safety I have ever had the pleasure of playing with, was so funny. Just an upbeat person who helped me understand the remarkable power of laughter, Guss showed me that it could be fuel for the soul and energy for the spirit. He really played a major role in me getting over a minor complex I had about the size of my head. I'm a big person and my face is no different. As a kid, I was always picked on for my large dome and, as you probably know, nothing is off limits on a football team. I was a little self-conscious about it all...until I met Guss.

This may sound somewhat harsh, but Guss had a way of making everyone feel the same by making fun of all of us, himself included. I'll never forget Guss telling Ciatrick

Fason he looked like Darrell Lee with hair and the two of them staring at each other and slowly realizing it was true. Those few seconds were absolutely hilarious. Guss kept it light, kept it real and kept everyone going. Right away, he was the best football player of us all as well. I still don't think there has been a better safety at Florida.

Darrell, or as I sometimes call him "D-Lee", was about as straightforward as they come. He was honest when things were good and honest when things were bad. If there was something that needed to be said, Darrell said it. If there was something that didn't need to be said, Darrell probably said that, too. The reality was that all of us needed that reality-check. Long before the phrase "keeping it 100", Darrell was the voice of the obvious in every single room. He kept things in perspective, all while keeping it fun.

Through all of the craziness that surrounded and tried to consume us, Darrell, the number one defensive end recruit in the country coming out of high school, kept our heads from reaching the clouds. Even mine. Darrell also kept our feet on the ground. Whenever someone offered up a wild idea or slanted view, he was there to check them. I guess when you're basically bald your whole life as he was, you just have to keep it simple across the board. Something else I will always remember about Darrell is that he was a really good dancer. He could get it. When the liquid courage kicked in, D-Lee really got right. He also could have probably been a professional bowler.

I can say this being from a town like Swainsboro: Ronald Dowdy was country. Not a redneck, a "blackneck". Not only was he, like me, a little less refined and a little less cultured than some of the other guys on the team, he made sure everyone knew it. Ron, from Fayetteville, North Carolina, made me take even more pride in where I was from because he walked around with such pride in who and how he was.

Ron loved hunting and he probably had gone 1,000 times by the time I had met him. During our years in college, I never heard a single story about him ever actually killing anything, though. We all loved Gainesville, but Ron loved being out and about in those nearby small towns like Archer, Starke, Waldo and Williston. Channing Crowder, from Atlanta, and Brian Crum, from Camden County in deep south Georgia, were two more country boys who used to go fishing at nearby Lake Alice. Even they were nothing compared to Ron.

Carlos, or "Los" for short, was and remains an original. Now a pastor in the northeast, he has a captivating story. Carlos' family came to the United States from the Dominican Republic, so he had to adjust to a different culture as a grade-schooler. English, for his family, was a second language. Carlos once told me he learned how to speak it by watching *Sesame Street*. It's quite the introduction to America to think about now, but when Carlos told me that, with our house full of jokesters, I kindly chuckled and advised him to keep that to himself. Carlos helped me learn about the world and was sort of my starting point for understanding different perspectives.

As his current profession indicates, Carlos is a devout Christian. Transitioning to adulthood, much less playing major college football, can be a tricky time in one's life. No matter what I was going through, Carlos, who even preached some in college, was always there to reinforce my faith. He was my guardian angel, was and remains my spiritual compass and reminded me of just how good God was to me. Also, how God sends you the people you need. Carlos is my Dominican faith brother.

So much of what we did everyday was done together. We formed a bonus brotherhood that went well beyond the team. We leaned on each other, relied on each other and a magical bond came from that. Each of our own life milestones had at least some tie to one another.

One memory that comes to mind is when Carlos, who was dating his future wife, bought a bear for her that was about six feet tall. This thing was huge. He was so proud of it and was so excited to give it to her. When he was about to go back home to New Jersey, we all actually convinced him that the bear had to ride in a seat on the plane because of how big it was and that he had to buy an extra ticket. That was our way of showing love.

When Guss was playing for the Houston Texans early in his NFL career, Darrell, from Missouri, Kirkwood to be exact, actually went back out west and lived with him. Guss had a couple of siblings, Boogie, Boo, Red and Dominique, with him. Darrell slid right in just like he was family. Because he was. Darrell started working in Houston, actually met his wife there and still lives in Houston to this day.

There were obviously other guys on the team who I very much enjoyed being around and got to spend some extra time with. Kenny Parker from Warner Robins, Georgia was yet another country boy suddenly in the Sunshine State. He is now a big-time college football strength and conditioning coach. One thing I remember is how much Kenny loved ketchup. Bennie Mills from Metairie, Louisiana was incredibly smart and loved playing video games, which always made me laugh.

I lived with O.J. Small early on, then Kelvin Kight and Travis Harris. Those boys were all great and I benefited from being around each of them. O.J. had a cool personality and helped me de-stress a lot just by being himself. I have to call him out for his basketball jumper, though, as it had absolutely no arc. It was a shotput. All of the ladies loved Kelvin and Travis, aka "T-Easy". Kelvin is an accomplished salesman and Travis, who was career-oriented when he was 18 years old, is another successful businessman. Both were smooth dudes with confidence that seamlessly turned into swagger. I tried to take notes. I have always admired all of those boys, even to this day.

It felt like so much was happening every single day early in my career at Florida. From meeting new people to watching how their choices impacted mine, my head was constantly spinning.

For every action, there is an equal or opposite reaction. Forget Sir Isaac Newton, all of my coaches were constant examples of that. When something happened to one of us, all of us, in some shape or form, felt it. The ripple effect of decisions that expand through a team is considerable.

My freshman year, we had an offensive guard named Earnest Smith who randomly missed practice one day. That was unheard of. Coach Spurrier, usually calm and relaxed, got really serious and told Earnest, who was a big -time recruit out of Jacksonville, that if he missed practice again he would be kicked off the team. Earnest called Coach Spurrier's bluff and skipped practice once more. I never saw Earnest again.

How that impacted us, in addition to the team losing a talented player, is that Earnest was roommates with Guss Scott. Though just a freshman, Guss, because of that, ended up with his own room. We spent a lot of time there from that point on.

Beyond Guss having some extra space at home, I learned accountability from the story of Earnest Smith. It was unfortunate for him, but the way Coach Spurrier responded was a stark reminder of the seriousness of what we were all doing. That the choices we made, individually and as a group, had consequences. Whether we admitted it at the time or not, the rest of us in the class of 2000 got a wake-up call from that news. There is a time and a place for everything. If you are a college football player, that time and place is exactly when and where the coaches say.

Especially if it was the head coach. Especially if it was Steve Spurrier. There was a learning process in the classroom, in the community and on the field. It applied to all of us indiscriminately. My crew stuck together as a sponge and absorbed everything we went though, blood, sweat and tears, together.

One of the neat aspects of being around the same people every day is that by copying some of their words and phrases, mimicking some of their style and implementing some of their strengths, you all mold each other like pieces of wet clay. That was the case with me and my roommates and me and my Fab Five. On the same path, our steps ultimately became one and the same.

We all grew in that way, with the circumstances and responsibilities around us making us even more tight-knit. It was a different type of peer pressure. My friends became a mosaic of me and me a mosaic of them. In the most literal of ways, those guys deserve credit for me ever staying, much less succeeding, at Florida.

I needed Guss to help me get over my own insecurities. I needed Darrell to help me see through all of the nonsense. I needed Ron to remind me that I needed to be myself. I needed Carlos to help reinforce my faith. Like *Captain Planet* drawing on the forces of the *Planeteers*, I needed the earth, water, wind and fire to find my heart. Those around you can prompt an inner strength inside of you to develop. That was definitely the case for me.

Even as I try to explain it, the guys I've mentioned will never know just how much they meant to me and continue to mean to me. My story was intertwined with each of their stories. We figured it all out side-by-side, football and life. We maintained those bonds as young adults, relationships that were equally as valuable.

One truth that I wish humanity would embrace and talk about more is how much all of us, regardless of gender or race, money or fame, really need each other. Every person is connected and, big picture, love in the world starts with how we treat and care for those closest to us. It's never okay to leave anyone behind. I developed a "least among us" mentality with Sister Christine Peeples in Swainsboro, one which went on to evolve at Florida. Guss, Darrell, Ron and Carlos are all responsible for that continuation.

I don't talk about this much, but, as mentioned, I didn't have many friends growing up. I was blessed to have a large and tight-knight family, but I was always careful and cautious, distrusting even, outside of it. As I got older and progressed in school, I didn't seek out others like most of my peers did. My brother Lucus and Titus Peeples and I were the original crew and that was more than I ever needed. We did everything together, barely leaving each other's side. As a teenager, my social interactions didn't go much further than them.

Not only did I not have a lot of friends who were guys, I was very inexperienced when it came to the ladies. I showed up on Florida's campus a virgin. To this very day, I don't know if that was a secret or not, but my boys never treated me any differently.

As long as I can remember, I have been a loner, at peace in mostly avoiding others. Quite honestly, it was going to be difficult for me to settle in as a high-profile college football player, much less make it in the NFL, without expanding my horizons and becoming much more comfortable around people I initially didn't know. When I say I needed the Fab Five, I really mean it.

I also needed my big brother. Though stubborn and hard-headed as it gets, Lucus has always been there for me. And he was still there for me when I was at Florida, despite him being on the other side of the world. Lucus joined the United States Marines after high school, a feat I never could have accomplished. Not long after, he was deployed overseas, doing very dangerous work that gave me the freedom to do the very frivolous things I was doing. He did multiple tours of duty, showing bravery, commitment and selflessness in serving our country at home and abroad.

Lucus served in North Africa and the Middle East and was specifically in Mosul, Iraq with the 26th Marine Expeditionary Unit as part of S-6 Radio, also attached to the VMGR-252 helicopter unit, while I was in Gainesville. He was always on my mind, in my thoughts and in my prayers. I know it was especially difficult for my parents to have him off at war. While I was off at college, I used to talk with my mother about Lucus and all that he was caught up in. Sometimes I didn't know what to say.

A newspaper did an article on Lucus and I, titling it with a play on words with our last name. Reading about what I was doing compared to what he was doing only reinforced some of the feelings I was having; I was playing a game, while he was off living in the desert and was working in life-and-death situations every day. It was very difficult for me to ignore all of that.

People were calling me a hero, but Lucus, and others like him, really were. It never truly felt right that I was receiving the attention and acclaim, given where Lucus was and what he was doing.

The terrorist attacks of 9/11 happened while I was at Florida and while Lucus was preparing to go to Iraq. He actually helped with the humanitarian assistance with the Marines who were going to New York to respond. That tragedy impacted our game schedule, but that obviously was absolutely irrelevant in comparison to what was happening in New York City, Washington D.C. and overseas. The entire world was on pause.

I will never forget walking into one of the buildings on campus and trying to piece together all that I was seeing. Later in life I was able to visit the 9-11 Memorial in Manhattan, an experience that I can't describe. I am in awe of how so many people, all of them heroes, responded to help others that day.

After the horror of 9/11, our game against Tennessee was actually rescheduled for December. In those times, though, what we were or weren't doing didn't matter. What my brother was doing very much did. His safety was always on my mind. So was his sacrifice.

In addition to Lucus being my family and us having an everlasting love, I greatly appreciate his service. I will always have a special place in my heart and a special appreciation for all who serve. My brother followed in our daddy's footsteps. Regardless of if he was with us and driving the backroads of east Georgia or if he was thousands of miles away watching my games at odd hours of the night, Lucus has been a leading part of every crew I have ever had.

Albeit in a different way, that was definitely the case during my playing career. I talked about Lucus with Guss, Darrell, Ron and Carlos all the time. And Lucus, always my biggest fan, supported the Gators and the Titans wherever he went. He was talking trash to people who didn't even speak English. Though I wish I was able to share some of my achievements with him more directly, there was something special about him being so involved from so far away.

While my friends helped me get through all that was going on around me, Lucus fought for the freedom I had to do it. My brother has been and will always be one of the greatest among us. That Troupe boy is a bad boy. Family, after all, is a crew that always sticks and stays together.

I was fortunate to find a new family similar to mine in Gainesville. One of my great friends at Florida was Ashley Moore, the sister of Gator royalty Terry and Willie Jackson was one of the strongest I had around campus. Their mother Delphine treated me like I was one of the boys. She opened up their house to me.

Willie, Jr. still doesn't know this, but I literally used to borrow and wear his shoes and take them back-and-forth from their family home. To say I humbly followed in his footsteps is an understatement. I also used to eat up all of his strawberry ice cream from the refrigerator, another fact that he may not know. I can vividly imagine him coming home, opening up the door in the kitchen and angrily wondering where it all went.

One of Florida's best players ever and an NFL star, Willie was always so generous with his time. He constantly talked to me about life beyond football and always stopped to visit every time he saw me. He also never called me "Ben", rather "Troupe". Willie was so personable to me. Simply-speaking, Willie was a stand up dude who would always share his wisdom. I still appreciate that.

Another Gator great, Terry, who won a national championship in Gainesville, furthered those sentiments as he helped me see the value of becoming an intellectual. Terry was also a man of his word. One time in college, he borrowed ten dollars from me. I, having forgotten all about it, saw him years later and he randomly came up to me and returned the bill. That says a lot about who he is.

Willie and Terry's father is the incomparable pioneer Willie Jackson, Sr., the first African-American to play in a football game at Florida

Ashley was another little sister to me, even though I'm just slightly younger than her. She gave me context and helped keep me level headed in Gainesville. With one brother who was an All-American, and another who won it all, she, having played basketball at Florida, had literally seen it all. Ashley gave me balance. She critically helped me understand the importance of making Florida fit me, not making me fit Florida. She was my compass. I am forever grateful to her and how she also helped me further realize I was both who I was and who I was becoming.

For my Fab Five, this woman was our sixth man. What the Jacksons taught me was the importance of accountability and purpose. I am forever indebted to them, Florida's first family.

They say if your circle doesn't elevate you, it's not a circle, it's a cage. Not only did my group elevate me, those people gave me influence, perspective and the ability to understand that being myself was all that I ever needed to be.

For all of those who helped me along my way, for Ronald Dowdy, Darrell Lee, Carlos Perez and Guss Scott, for the Jacksons and others, there is power in people. It takes a village to raise a child. It sometimes takes a crew to raise a man.

FINDING MY PURPOSE

One thing that always makes me shake my head is how I frequently hear about what the college experience is supposed to be like, how enlightening those four years can be and how so many individuals find themselves and lay out a roadmap for the future during their time on campus. All of that is true, of course, but it is rarely talked about as it pertains to student-athletes.

We are simply supposed to, "shut up and dribble," remember?

Fact is, many of us go through the college transformation at an even-accelerated pace. The second we arrive on campus, the expectations are already firmly in place. There is no drop period, especially for receivers and tight ends. Our schedules are absolutely overwhelming and our standard is unrelentingly high. Unlike those of our classmates, our results are also constantly on display for everyone to see.

Now I'm not complaining, as we all choose to compete athletically at a high-profile institution. Obviously, great benefits such as free tuition, free room and board, access to extra infrastructure and personal branding, just to name a few bonuses, accompany our rise. I just get frustrated when I hear others talk about the life-altering value college can have, but they don't ever seem to think that those same developments are happening with those of us who play a sport.

People, for whatever reason, don't seem to view us in that same regard. Let me set the record straight.

A lifelong passion of mine was cultivated at Florida. It wasn't football, rather through football, instead. That shouldn't come as a surprise to anyone, either. Not only do most of us learn specific lessons from the games we played, we developed other far-reaching interests as well. Some of us fell in love with coaching, the idea of teaching a sport we love to the next generation of athletes. Others, like I have, find their way into the media and end up on the other side of the same microphone they were once awkwardly speaking into.

In terms of careers related to athletics, there are former football players who become administrators, agents, health and fitness workers or referees. Additionally, there are countless indirect ways that what we experience ends up shaping what we do. Teamwork is a naturally transferable skill. I thank God everyday for what I did and saw at Florida and for the decades of service it helped stir inside of me.

I am my brother's keeper. That is a line that has always deeply resonated with me. The Bible says, "When I was a child I spoke as a child, I understood as a child, I thought as a child, but when I became a man I put away childish things." My time with the Gators helped me figure out how to put that passage to use. Beyond sports, all that I did helped me find myself and identify who I really was.

Even if we, sometimes young and aloof, don't realize it right away, one of the great benefits of being a student-athlete is that it introduces you to the gift of service. For many teenagers, these opportunities are our first to be part of a reading session, clean-up effort, building project or other community-based event. These experiences for me really opened up my eyes at Florida and helped me see how many people need an outstretched hand. They helped me realize that I was capable of making a difference.

It was like a light was flipped on inside my brain. Suddenly I saw others suffering and also saw that I, Ben Troupe, from little old Swainsboro, Georgia, could be an advocate, a strong back or a comforting friend. More than any single play or any one game, that revelation, when I was still a very young man, made an impact on me that was truly inspirational. It changed my life. It did so by lighting a spark.

As student-athletes, we have certain projects that we are required to be involved with. It shouldn't be that way as we should all want to take part, but sometimes, as was the case with me, you need a little push. A kick in the butt, even. Early in my career and early in my life, I had no idea of the impact I could make on people. Though it took some time, I'm so grateful I finally found out.

On my journey to a better understanding of the human condition, however, I admittedly did not get off on the right foot. When my name came up on the volunteer-list twice in a few weeks, I actually went to Coach Zook to ask him why. That, too, went about as well as you would have expected. He used some different choice words and truly creative and descriptive phrasing in his impassioned response to me. Coach Zook explained that I was "getting to", not "having to," take part in these civic engagements. Yet again, Coach Zook was 100% right. In that moment, I learned that you become more by doing more.

It was me who needed the attitude adjustment. It turned out to be the most important one I have ever received. My road to selflessness had begun.

The popularity of our football team came with an incredible power around town, one that I wasn't fully aware of at first. I obviously knew that SEC football was very popular and that Florida, with a national championship in the recent rear-view, was and remains as big of a name as there is in college sports. That said, I honestly did not know that the simplest of gestures from somebody like me, just another member of the team, could make a lasting impression on somebody else. It was truly humbling. It was a gift, one of my circumstances and relative fame, that I suddenly wanted to make sure I was using to positively influence as many people as possible.

Remarkably, we were able to change moods and brighten days and do so by sharing just a few minutes of our time. When we showed up places, it really meant a lot to people, some of whom were really struggling and needed a proverbial pat on the back. When you are 19 or 20 years old, it can be hard to see the greater good in most of the things you do. These experiences, helping me see more than merely myself, served as my mirror and window alike.

Appreciation, for me, at that point, was lacking. Through those incredible interactions and unique experiences, my understanding of appreciation was now starting to form.

As a young man, I always felt like there was a little something missing in my life. Some potential that wasn't quite being fulfilled. The smiles of the people we were helping helped me find mine. They helped me feel completely fulfilled. Along the way, I realized that I was actually the one being inspired.

At my first few volunteer outings, I wasn't quite sure what to say. So I simply started listening. Once I felt more comfortable and engaged, I became the one learning from those I was there to talk to. While football sometimes felt a little out of place, I quickly felt at home in the rooms of strangers. It was as if I was reborn once again and given a tool I didn't even know existed. There was so much more for me to learn. Whenever Coach Zook heard any of us say that we were football players, he would correct us and explain that we were people who played football. I was finally starting to understand.

"To much is given, much is required." I was motivated, inspired and ready to work. I was eager to do my part. I didn't know it at first, but I was discovering my purpose.

My interactions on various service projects, starting with visits to nearby Shands Hospital on campus, were truly profound. The importance of those trips will forever remain. In addition to spending some time interacting with sick kids, which was very eye-opening and emotional in itself, I was able to meet with their families and loved ones. Outside of me trying to spread some genuine positivity, I was also able to offer a listening ear, some personal support and even a little thankful feedback. My view of the world was changing.

A whole new perspective was opening up. A whole new set of priorities came with it. For the first time, my love for football was being challenged by something different.

I continued to be regularly involved with volunteer work while at Florida and couldn't stop thinking about what more could be done. Our bowl game trips served as extensions of all of my experiences. I was introduced to more, got to take part in things I wouldn't have otherwise gotten to and did so in places where I wouldn't have otherwise been.

When I hear pundits talk about how there are too many bowl games, I wish more people understood all of the opportunities that they present. Bowl trips are a comprehensive reward, much more than merely 60 minutes of extra football. I played in the Orange Bowl, the Sugar Bowl and the Outback Bowl twice. Who we played against and whether or not we won is only part of what I remember.

Miami and Tampa, Florida and New Orleans, Louisiana are three of the most recognizable cities in the entire United States. Visiting those places and seeing the attractions were important pit-stops in my personal maturation. Traveling and seeing other areas is a great way to learn about culture and realize that not everybody lives or thinks the same way that you do. From local food and entertainment to city design and layout, each town I went to during my football career was different. So, too, were their needs.

A defining aspect of any bowl trip is the community work each team does. A part of the scheduled itinerary for both sides are shared trips to local hospitals, youth homes or military bases, volunteer appointments that were mutually-beneficial to both parties. Before the actual game, they serve as a collective priority to help the underprivileged, uplift the struggling or recognize those who are sacrificing. We learned as we served. Those experiences were inspiring for everybody involved. They were deeply meaningful to me.

I found something that made me feel like I mattered outside of football. What I felt was more powerful than anything I ever felt on the field. My love for philanthropy and people was firmly cemented.

From that point, my passion for service grew right alongside my career. I became even more invested and involved in the Gainesville community and, upon being drafted by the Tennessee Titans, was excited and eager to do the same in Nashville. I felt like volunteerism, not just football, was my calling. My personal responsibility. Needless to say, I took that with me everywhere I went and I still do. I continue to be affirmed by other people, empowered by their stories and honored, to my core, to play a very small part in making the world a better place.

Every single one of us have that amazing, God-given ability. We can positively impact everyone we meet. The more we focus on the least among us, the better we all become. When I donate or show up, I don't do so only to help others; I do it to change me as well. I have to continue to remind myself of the importance of every single person, every single situation and make sure that my actions consistently reinforce those ideas. Just as I wouldn't stop practicing for football once I reached a certain threshold, I won't stop working for others just because I've done it a few times.

More, here, is the only measure. Doing my part is the goal. Shining my light so that others can see what drives me.

Not only am I my brother's keeper, I am my brother. I have always considered myself to be a regular person and consider all of us, regardless of address or occupation, to be both the same and the same way. When I see others hurt, I feel it. I also genuinely take pride in the accomplishments of the people I'm around. Some of my favorite memories as a football player were watching my teammates succeed. We share the glory and the pain, on the field and off.

One of my biggest frustrations is when those commonalities aren't maintained, respected or upheld. Or, at the very least, acknowledged.

While football has given me a platform, all of us, myself included, can do meaningful work from the ground-up. Sometimes it's unseen, but that can be when and where acts are the most impactful. The chances to strengthen our communities, help people without a clear path towards upward mobility and appreciate those who are working towards a better tomorrow are all within our reach. That change, in terms of how we think, how we act and how we live, is inside of us. We all can act on it.

We owe it to each other to be the friend we want our neighbor to be. False narratives are largely fixed when searching for truth. When I see abandoned houses, down-trodden areas or hear of young people without the resources to expand their horizons, it makes me sad. It also makes me wonder. What can we do to raise the floor in America? A rising tide is supposed to lift all boats.

I still have a thirst for service that cannot be quenched. And I went to the school where Gatorade was invented.

I have been so comprehensively rewarded in having had a wide-range of volunteer interactions. Every single one of them has deeply enriched my life. I simply would not be the same person without them. Perhaps my most profound experience was when I traveled to Haiti as a part of a multi-organizational trip with numerous non-profits. I honestly had not seen anything like that before, the destruction and poverty that followed the earthquake of 2010.

Haiti is a beautiful country with lovely people, but the nation lacked many of the amenities and some of the infrastructure we have in the United States. That was especially the case after such a devastating natural disaster.

Strikingly, I was amazed at how the residents made the absolute most of their surroundings and how they persevered through the adversity that I saw when I was there. As is the case with everything I have been fortunate to do, traveling to Haiti, on the same large island as the Dominican Republic, where Carlos Perez is from, helped me expand my worldview. This was true literally and figuratively.

In addition to learning about a captivating new culture, I felt the rare fragility of situations many of us are able to take for granted every single day. What I saw moved me. It was a real-life example of the theory of relativity. Even the most humble part of my upbringing paled in comparison to the difficulty I was only very briefly around in Haiti.

Through that unfortunate strife, my passion grew even more. I consistently saw people going above and beyond for others. I saw children laughing and playing. I felt an enthusiasm for community that, even in difficult circumstances, was very much there. It was an in-my-face reminder of the magic of the human spirit. The more we all talked, the more I resonated with the Haitian people and the more they resonated with me. I have an everlasting love for them.

We played their version of football and even talked a little American football, though every single person I met seemed to think I played for the New York Giants. Jeremy Shockey, I was not; shocked, however, I very much was.

Part of what struck me was the sheer desperation. I couldn't shake it. So many people were in so much need. As soon as I got off the plane, hands were reaching through a chain-link fence reaching for money. People were chasing me and pulling at me as I walked through town, asking for any and everything I had. It wasn't uncomfortable, just unsettling; the idea that the hat I was wearing was an item that another person wanted so badly, merely so they could cover their head from the sun, was sobering.

I ended up giving away the beads I was wearing, the shoes on my feet and some extra things I had in my bag. I still wish I had more and was able to do more.

Even though most of the residents spoke a version of Haitian Creole, some spoke limited or broken English and I was able to talk with many people. I learned so much. I was even called out by a child in an exchange that helped remind me where I was. This boy asked me if there were poor people in America. I nodded in affirmation and, before I could expand on saying yes, he interrupted me. He asked me, honestly and innocently, if those poor people had houses, had water, had clothes and had food. He then pulled on his school clothes and told me, in his way, that what he had on was all he had.

There is true poverty everywhere, including in America. That child was showing me just how tragically dire his unique situation was.

There were moments like those that really made me think. We were eating dinner at a restaurant inside the hotel where we were staying. During our meal, the inside power suddenly went out. All of us Americans either paused abruptly or shrieked, while the locals just kept right on eating. You could literally tell where everybody was from just by how they reacted. At that point after the earthquake, much of Haiti was running on generators. Modest inconveniences like the lights going out were no reason to even put down your fork.

Nights later, we went to a local bar. Upon leaving and casually walking down one of the roads, I heard a voice, not able to see this person, cautiously whispering to me, "Don't go down there, don't go down there". Needless to say, I did not. Where I was truly came with a different reality.

I kept getting asked the same question, regardless of what village or neighborhood I was visiting: when would I be coming back? The people I met in Haiti were so appreciative, warm and welcoming. They were passionate in sharing their stories with newcomers like me. Knowing that I had to leave soon, each time I was asked it tugged at my heart. These people didn't know me from anybody else, but I was there for them and that meant a lot. I served as a representation of some form of hope, an example of compassion and the embodiment of the rare opportunity that America represents.

To all my friends in Haiti, I will be back. I promise. *Mwen renmen ak manke ou. Mwen pral we ou anko byento.*

A seed that was planted during my time at Florida has grown into a vibrant flower. It represents the beauty I see in others. In addition to my start at Shands, I have been honored to work with such awe-inspiring national non-profit groups as the Make-A-Wish Foundation, St. Jude's Hospital, Read to America, the Boys & Girls Club, the YMCA and Head's Up Football. I have been blessed to speak to students in Alabama, California, Connecticut, Florida, Georgia, Massachusetts, New Jersey, New York, North Carolina, Ohio, South Carolina and Tennessee. I was humbled to talk to hundreds of soldiers from the 3rd Infantry Division, among them my friend John Thomas Bennett, at Fort Stewart mere days before they shipped off to Afghanistan.

It has been my pleasure to also work with local grass-roots organizations like the League of Brawn, the volunteer extension of the Chatham County Sheriff's Office, Hearts for Heroes, the Cpl. John Stalvey Foundation and the African American Male Initiative at East Georgia College. Sometimes underfunded and overlooked, there are thousands of groups like these around the country that do God's work in helping to change lives for the better. They do so without any fame or recognition. My hat goes off to all of them.

Even more so than any of my football accomplishments, it has been one of my biggest joys in life to watch my father now share his message with those who may be currently caught up in the same mistakes he used to make through his non-profit group Men Reaching Men. As is the case with me, my daddy has now found his purpose. He is the perfect man for the job. All of us are at our best when we are doing what we love. John Troupe is currently thriving.

Every person has that potential. Often, we choose not to make the most of it. Helping others can take a few short seconds of your life. How many times have we all driven by a family with a broken down car stranded on the side of the road? How many times have we seen someone put items back after receiving their total at the check-out line? How many times have we looked right past someone holding up a sign asking for money or asking for food? How many times have we known that our neighbors were struggling but decided that it wasn't our problem? How many times have we stopped and asked ourselves what we can do for somebody else?

What if we or someone we love were that person in need? Think about how much better the world would be if we only acted as if. How we treat the least among us tells us a lot about ourselves.

People will forever associate me with the University of Florida through football and I am forever grateful for that. Year-in and year-out, the Gators showcase some of the most talented players and coaches in the country and the product is one every fan should be proud of. I certainly am. That said, so much of my personal foundation was laid in Gainesville. The start of my building process took place there.

My biggest takeaway from Florida was, whether on a team or in the community, how much we all need each other. The answer is one and the same.

When I speak to groups or visit with people now, I often think about who I was when I arrived on campus. How young I was. How inexperienced I was. How naive I was. I needed everything I experienced to help me make an early transition to adulthood. I needed those first couple of visits to Shands. I needed Coach Zook reminding me of the value of those interactions. I needed a reality check, even if it was first signed by somebody else.

It was Florida that forced me in the right direction. Graciousness is what I took from "Gator Nation". I came to Gainesville hungry. I left full, with so much extra I wanted to share.

As was the case with Jamie McClouskey and his couch at Florida, these are the unseen developments that come with college football. Every player is a person with a story. Each one of us is impacted in some way or somehow by challenges well beyond football. I deeply understand the attraction and celebration that every game is, but I hope that, through all of the pomp and circumstance, we don't lose sight of the fact that these are young men, many of them teenagers, making a staggering amount of progress that goes much further than just ten yards at a time.

Football has a way of dehumanizing people. We can't lose sight of who is playing these games. I want those considerations to be kept in mind whenever we talk about student-athletes and harp on their success or failure. Context is everything and there is a lot going on here. It's important to remember that there is a face behind each facemask. The shoulders under each set of shoulder pads already have more on them than most will ever know.

When we talk about a player's body of work, it's okay to remember the heart and soul as well. For all of the aspects of the game that I love, my goal is to help some of those stigmas change, just as I individually did during my time with the Gators.

When I think about those now going through what I did, bettering themselves away from the field while working hard on it, they all have my admiration. I respect and appreciate all of them. Playing college football is an all-day, every-day grind. You have to balance rigorous academics with the spotlight of being at least a local-celebrity and do so while competing with and against some of the most talented players in the country.

Between it all, you somehow learn a little something. Not just in the classroom, either. You learn about other people. You learn about yourself. You learn about life. With so much exposure, hopefully you have the time to process everything coming your way.

I will always remember winning an SEC Championship, running on the field in the Orange Bowl and my catch over Thomas Davis. Those moments, as great as they were, didn't necessarily shape me as much as they shaped the outside perception of me. Going to Shands changed my perspective. All of the volunteer work I am grateful to do now still does.

Win or lose, I was exactly the same person before and after every football game I played. I was not the same person after those visits to hospitals, needy areas or schools. These were moments that changed me.

Florida was my springboard forward for football, which turned out to be my first career. With that came money and opportunity that I would have had a difficult time replicating on my own. Florida was also my pathway to a passion. Without the Gators showing me the way, I'm not sure I ever would have been as complete of a person as I feel I am today.

I was introduced to a lot at Florida, most notably the man I always hoped I would be. As long as I can remember, I have had a servant's heart. In college, I found out how to follow it.

GOING PRO

I've been asked countless times why I was selected 40th in the 2004 NFL Draft by the Tennessee Titans. My honest answer to this day is: I have no idea.

I don't know what separated me from the rest. All I know is that my agent, the great Joel Segal, told me a few days before it started that I would not go lower than 40th overall. Maybe he spoke it all into existence. It honestly took me a while to fully realize that I was a top prospect. Even though all of my paths were starting to lead to the next level, I never felt like all that I was experiencing was a guarantee of any professional opportunity.

Some guys talk about how reaching the NFL was always a lifelong goal. For me, it was barely a fleeting thought.

After the Outback Bowl my junior season, when I surprisingly started to get some questions about the possibility of turning pro, that is when I really started to think about the potential of playing at football's highest level. Following Rex Grossman's decision to enter the NFL Draft, I saw him around the football facility not long after and he asked me if I was ready for what was coming. At the time, I didn't know what he was even talking about. In retrospect, I truly had no idea.

Throughout my senior year, with me catching 39 passes for 638 yards and five touchdowns and earning first-team All-American honors, things really started to take shape. After my final game, it all suddenly became a blur. The pre-draft process happened so fast, with constant media attention and speculation, that it seemed surreal. In the beginning, I was completely and utterly overwhelmed.

Even though I had played my last game for the Gators, I still needed the folks at Florida to help me get off and running in my new direction. From my coaches to compliance and sports information staff members, they helped me do just that. Mike Spiegler and Ashley Bowman Brouillette, who most players simply went to for game tickets, were close advisors of mine. They were critical in helping me through the most important part of my transition: picking my agent. They both also helped constantly remind me that I was so much more than what I did on Saturdays or might do on Sundays. To them, I was a person, one who just happened to play football. That meant a lot.

I officially knew the draft was real when "Spieg" told me that every pro prospect had a professional binder, but that I had two of them. Years later, he was actually at my Florida-Georgia Hall of Fame banquet. At the 2019 game in Jacksonville, we were sitting right next to each other in the stadium press box. He didn't see me as we were separated by plexiglass. I wanted to excitedly bang on it and get his attention. Spieg and Ashley went far beyond what their job required and helped make my college experience complete.

Before I really got into the thick of draft preparation, I needed someone to guide me through it. Potential contractual details aside, the transition from college to the NFL can be a thick jungle of events and interviews, a daily reinvention of who you are and what you do. Anticipating that chaos, which advisors were telling me was undoubtedly coming, my family and I scheduled meetings with agents on campus.

Enter Joel Segal. Though I was impressed with the professionalism of everyone I sat down with, including the late Eugene Parker, who is considered the godfather of African-American representation and helped open doors for the long-list of minority agents excelling today, there was something different and distinct about Joel. It was his informality that actually appealed to me. While all of the other agents understandably showed up in suits and ties, Joel arrived differently, in a t-shirt and jeans. He was casually simple and straightforward.

Joel told me, to my face, that he wouldn't be in Gainesville unless I had the chance to be a top pick. That the trip wouldn't be worth his time. Those were refreshing realities that I could appreciate. Joel was relaxed, but real. He was cool, but confident. He had some similarities to Coach Spurrier. Maybe it was fate, but Joel also called me "Bennie".

The way Joel carried himself and the genuine way he presented his vision to me and my family made me feel like I could trust him and let him lead me into this next chapter of my life. I'm glad I did.

Eyes wide open, I immediately went down to New Orleans to work with well-known trainer Tom Shaw. My plan was to be as prepared as possible and to hit every pre-draft milestone marker: the Senior Bowl, the NFL Combine and my pro day. I had momentum stemming from a big game in my regular season finale against Florida State, with four catches for 121 yards and two touchdowns. I also felt at ease with Joel calling some of the shots.

The idea behind going to Louisiana to work with Tom was simple; I had just had a productive year and met the size and athleticism prototype that most professional teams wanted, but I needed to prepare my body and mind for not only a higher level of competition, but a higher level of scrutiny as well. At Florida, I trained to be ready to face other teams. Now, I needed to train to be ready to face the critics.

Fair or not, the minutiae of what I ran in the forty yard dash, how many bench press repetitions I did or how detailed my footwork was in practice drills now came with the utmost of importance. Money was on the line. I needed Tom to help me better understand the nuance of new workouts. I was soon to be inspected like never before. Furthermore, everything I did would soon come with an evaluation. After years of As and Bs, this grading system was set to be completely different. Numbers, this time, those with lots of zeros, could be following my name.

Whether comfortable with the distinction or not, I was about to be considered one of the best athletes on the planet. I needed to be prepared for all that came with that. I needed to be ready to look and play the part.

One of the neat aspects of being in New Orleans is that I was working with guys I used to compete against. Especially pre-social media and before the widespread growth of the recruiting circuit, I did not know much about the players on other rosters. Even guys who were in -conference or in-state. I ended up training with some outstanding athletes, stars like Michael Boulware, Greg Jones and Stanford Samuels from Florida State, Ahmad

"Batman" Carroll from Arkansas and even some playmakers from outside of the region like Michael Jenkins from Ohio State and Chris Perry from Michigan.

It was comforting, in a way, to have other prospects there to relate to, many of whom had personal stories very similar to mine. Regardless of where we played in college, we formed a bond on the bayou. It was forged in the unrelenting heat and humidity of the Pelican State, countless hours spent finding ourselves while sweating some of it out as well. We earned every repetition we did. I respect all of those boys. I needed them to help shape my perspective. We were all going through the same thing and working towards the same thing. We were in it together.

Each of us had one eye on the future and one eye on the past. We were anxious for what was upcoming, using only what we had individually accomplished in college as our framework for the future. One night a bunch of us were out at dinner and Dexter Reid from North Carolina showed up. Now Dexter was a great player and would actually go on to win a pair of Super Bowls, but he didn't know what, or who, he was running into all over again.

Among the guys at our table was Greg Jones, a bruising 250-pound running back who would move to fullback in the NFL. Greg looked like the Incredible Hulk. Unfortunately, for Dexter, one of Greg's Florida State highlights came against the Tar Heels on a play where he got out into the flat and ran, with a full head of steam, into a much smaller North Carolina defensive back. It did not go well for the out-of-position safety, who Greg stiff-armed, lifted and decleated into the back of another blocking receiver in Chris Davis, who I would actually go on to play with in

Tennessee. That sequence was a signature play for Greg, with Dexter, of all people, on the receiving end.

Nobody realized all of this at first, with us all simply sitting down and ordering food. After a few minutes, though, Batman started to figure it all out and broke the ice with the simple-but-sly question with a grin, "wait a minute, aren't you the guy who…?" It all turned to laughter thankfully, with Greg and Dexter both smiling and sharing their sides of the story.

While innocent, the harshness of that moment would be a lesson for us all. We were about to enter into a stretch of our lives where there would be nowhere to hide.

Step one, out into a brave new world, was going to be the Senior Bowl. An annual scouting combine held in Mobile, Alabama, it has become an important part of the pre-draft process. In addition to an actual game that is held, the week offers a critical few days of one-on-one and unit-specific practices, direct engagement with prospects and NFL coaches and administrators, along with media opportunities. Players must settle into a different type of spotlight there.

Though I was excited to get my feet wet, I was also somewhat nervous and uneasy. Not because I didn't think I could compete, rather I was dealing with a dislocated finger. I was in a difficult spot because I was ready to get after it and showcase my talents, but was honestly worried about being limited, even if just some, by my injury. I wanted to make sure I was going to be able to put my best foot forward. Especially with money potentially at play.

Regardless of what decision I made, there was a chance it might be received poorly. It could even hurt my reputation and, in terms of a falling draft stock, cost me dearly.

Especially when you are a potential high draft pick, every move or moment is overanalyzed. That is where Tom Shaw stepped in. As a highly-respected and well-known workout guru, he called the Senior Bowl on my behalf and explained my situation. He did that for two reasons. First, he is a good guy who cares for the athletes he works with. Second, he knew that I wouldn't simply take his word for it that I didn't have to go, that I needed to hear it from the brass in Mobile. Senior Bowl representation told Tom that I did not need to come if I wasn't fully healthy.

I was disappointed at my final decision to not attend the Senior Bowl, but that phone call helped put me at ease. If I'm being honest, I wouldn't have been at my best in Mobile because my mind was all over the place, too.

It seems silly to say now, but I honestly didn't do much deep reflection during the pre-draft process. There wasn't enough time to. So much of my focus was goal oriented; accomplish this task, then move onto the next one. Part of what makes the NFL so consuming is that the work it requires simply doesn't leave much time left for you to stop and think. And that is before you even get there. Before I ever took a professional snap, most of my days were already scheduled out with meticulous workout regimens, traveling and events.

In some ways, I think part of the design of the mad dash of the months that lead up to the draft is specifically created simply to get you accustomed to the work rate. Just like college teaches you the principles behind learning, everything you do before you sign with a professional team helps ease you into a professional role. There are layers to all of this.

Outside of the draft itself, the crown jewel of the NFL's off-season is without question the combine. Held in Indianapolis every year, the NFL Combine brings together the top 300-plus or so college prospects in the country, along with professional coaches, front office personnel, scouts and other evaluators for a multi-day smorgasbord of poking and prodding. The workouts, events and interviews are non-stop.

Paradoxically, combine results both matter and are blown way out of proportion. Though it is certainly important for potential high draft picks to meet a certain physical threshold as players are vying to compete against some of the premier athletes on the planet, the fact that the entire football-consuming community uses a few tenths-of-a-second of a forty yard dash time or a couple of extra repetitions on the bench press to reconfigure what years of game tape show is a little much. Let me actually call it what it really is: it's ridiculous. Football doesn't have a script.

Keep in mind, the environment at the combine is completely antiseptic. All of the drills are run crisply and cleanly, minus the chaos that actually makes the sport so difficult to play. Rarely, if ever, does any player run in a straight line for 40 consecutive yards in a football game, especially linemen. Never, either, does "weight room strength" come into play. The ability to respond to unforeseen circumstances is what matters in football. The ability to process information and do so in the blink of an eye.

It's worth noting that the drills don't even take into account the context of the basic minimums of competition, or the basic minimums of anything, period; the entire combine features young men wearing essentially nothing but their underwear. Think about that for a second...the most important interview of your career has you standing in your drawers in bright lights in front of a bunch of reporters. Welcome to the NFL.

That was one of the first revelations that stood out to me. I headed to Indianapolis nervous as, whether it should be this way or not, what you do there can make or cost you some serious money. What was striking is just how raw of a "meat market" the whole thing was. As a football player, you are used to being recognized by your height, weight and position, but this made me feel like I was going to be displayed next to the prime rib on a bed of ice in a glass window. Was I going to be drafted or delivered?

I realized in that moment that it didn't matter what I wanted; it was about what they wanted. I was becoming part of the shield and my last name was merely an identifier.

Before anything else, each of us had to drop down to nothing but our tea leaves and stand on stage in front of hundreds of onlookers to get our official height and weight measured. The fact that there were honest debates about our sizes leading up to all of this was wild, too. You would think that those metrics would be well-established facts by this point. One way or another, a half-inch here or there or ten extra or fewer pounds made a real difference to and for some.

While I was on stage, instructors were literally telling me to move and turn in different ways and when and how to bend my arms and legs. You can't make this stuff up. It's also hard to express exactly how you feel as a young black man standing in a room of mostly older white people telling you what to do. I was grateful to be going through these examinations as I knew what they represented, but something about the detail and direction of it all felt well out of place.

What brought the experience back to the center and helped me settle in was the camaraderie of all of the players there. Now you would think, given that we were all competing for a specific number of draft slots, that there would be an inherent level of animosity or selfishness. I did not feel that at all. The support in the room was actually inspiring. Guys were honestly rooting for each other and openly celebrating their results, even amongst their specific position groups. I guess all of us knew how hard it was to get to where we were. There was a meaningful mutual respect and appreciation.

That feeling of brotherhood mattered to me and helped me really enjoy most of what I went through. In some ways, it was an extension of what I felt at Florida. I roomed with a defensive end named Ronnie Ghant from Louisville, a school I genuinely thought about attending. He actually was from Lakeland, Florida, right outside of Gainesville. There was symmetry like that everywhere.

In addition to being there with nine of my Gator brothers in Ran Carthon, Dwayne Dixon, Kelvin Kight, Bobby McCray, Carlos Perez, Keiwan Ratliff, Guss Scott, Shannon Snell and Max Starks, along with the guys I had been training with, I remember seeing some of the star quarterbacks like Eli Manning from Ole Miss and Philip Rivers out of North Carolina State. Ben Roethlesberger from the other Miami was also there. Months later I would chat it up with those guys at the NFL's Rookie Premiere in Los Angeles.

From Pittsburgh's Larry Fitzgerald to Virginia Tech's DeAngelo Hall to Iowa's Bob Sanders to the late Miami legend Sean Taylor, true greats of the game were on hand. Many of them, I was able to meet for the first time. Some, like Darnell Dockett from Florida State, I knew of but actually got to know on a personal level. These were cool cats. They made me feel comfortable as we all shared a common bond.

There were some absolute freaks of nature on hand. One of my workout partners from New Orleans, Ahmad Carroll had one of the fastest forty times there with a 4.34. Batman was right behind my future teammate in Tennessee, Michael "The Rabbit" Waddle from North Carolina, with a combine-best 4.31. Bob Sanders was one of the stars of the show. At a rock-solid 5'8'', 204 pounds, he ran a 4.35 forty and had the highest vertical leap there at 41.5 inches. After he helped lock me down in the Outback Bowl, I had already seen all I needed to see. Sanders, who would go on to win Super Bowl XLI and be named the 2007 NFL Defensive Player of the Year, would later lacerate the spleen of one of my Titans teammates, my friend Bo Scaife.

Of the tight ends, Georgia's Ben Watson was downright superhuman. Somebody probably has pictures or videos of me saying "wow" each time he did something.

Ben, at 6'3'', 258 pounds, ran a 4.50 forty, had a 35.5-inch vertical and did 34 bench press reps of 225 pounds before promptly racking the weight himself. Just for point of reference, Ben was about as fast as Northern Illinois running back Michael "The Burner" Turner and about as strong as Miami nose guard Vince Wilfork.

Ben, for good measure, was the smartest person there as well. And I mean out of everyone, regardless of what their job was, in the entire building. He started out his career at Duke, before transferring, and tested a 48 out of 50 on the Wonderlic. It was one of the highest scores ever recorded at the combine. Ben actually told me he just didn't have time to finish the other two questions.

I did not do any of the events. Here is why. Joel and I discussed our plan before heading to Indianapolis and his view was that I was already regarded as one of the top tight ends on the board and the risk-reward angle for me simply was not very beneficial. If I worked out well, it would only validate the projections of me and would not be likely to boost my stock much. Conversely, if I did not perform up to expectations, I could lose momentum ahead of the stretch run entering the draft and literally lose money.

From a competitor's angle, that might sound counterintuitive. I badly wanted to compete, but I trusted Joel and trusted myself enough to know that I could rely on my tape. Remember, this was not a game, this was a business. A business that you constantly have to adjust to. While I didn't do any events at the combine, it still felt like I did everything there.

My upcoming pro day at Florida, performing in an environment where I would be more comfortable and working with quarterbacks and coaches I knew, would be where I would showcase my athletic measurables. The fact that Miami's Kellen Winslow, considered by many to be the top tight end available, also chose not to work out at the combine only confirmed the stance that Joel and I had.

Now, this did not mean that I went to the combine to sulk. What most fans don't realize is just how important the face time with NFL administrators can be. Combine interviews don't always make the national media cycles, but they can be as important as any workout result. Sometimes even more important. For the most part, these were some of our first direct interactions with our future employers.

Did we look others in the eyes? Were we confident with our answers? Did we seem like we wanted to be there? Everything we did, from how we carried ourselves to the general vibe we gave off, was being detailed and observed.

A lot of prospects understandably train for the psychological aspect of the NFL Combine, in addition to the physical testing. Maybe it was the Swainsboro, Georgia in me...I just tried to be myself. Sometimes that wasn't what people wanted to hear.

Mike Tice, the head coach of the Minnesota Vikings, got pissed with me because I told him that I didn't have any weaknesses on the football field. He didn't like that, but I was being truthful. And if I'm being honest, I had a who-the-hell-are-you mentality anyway. I wasn't being arrogant in the interview. I was just surprised that Coach Tice, in my opinion, was.

Make no mistake about it, some weird things happened as well. I think the teams do this on purpose to see how you will react. In one of the rooms where I was being interviewed, one of the coaches for the Tampa Bay Buccaneers was staring at me and eating Doritos. I thought it was all normal, until I realized he was eating them straight out of a metal desk drawer, with no bag or napkin or anything. He offered me some, which was nasty. Maybe if I would have eaten one they would have drafted me.

NFL legend Doug Williams was actually in the room with us. He and the tight ends coach were having a conversation about me right in front of me, as if I wasn't there. That was different.

Beyond that, one team even asked me how good Maryland's Fried Chicken was, the local fast food spot I ate at in Swainsboro as a kid. These teams know everything about you.

The Cleveland Browns had a psychologist present me with questions that I unfortunately had to answer. I was constantly asked such things as: "what kind of tree would I be", "what kind of animal would I be" and "how would I describe my personality?" One team asked me if I would rather be a star player on a losing team or a backup on a championship team? My response was simple: both. In terms of the psychobabble, I didn't dabble too much there. What you see is what you get with me.

Among other organizations, I felt very good about my meetings with Cleveland, Carolina and Green Bay. Mike Sherman, head coach of the Packers, even told me he would draft me in the first round if I was there when it was their turn to pick. Interestingly-enough, one team that I did not have an official meeting with was the Tennessee Titans. That is just the way it goes sometimes.

I do remember briefly visiting with Tennessee assistant coach George Henshaw, who would go on to become my position coach, in the hallway for a few short minutes. Maybe I made an impact. I had no sense at all that the Titans would be the team to select me. They chose me with their first draft pick that year, no less.

If I'm being truthful, in my heart I thought I was going to be picked by the Panthers. I just felt like there was some mutual interest there at the combine. It goes without saying that I'm grateful things worked out the way they did.

After the combine, what was happening was really starting to hit me. With regards to the NFL, I could finally see it and feel it. It was all anybody wanted to talk about. On my flight back from Indianapolis, one of the people sitting next to me was actually reading about me in a *Sporting News* magazine. He, too, seemed to know more about my future than I did.

This was the next iteration of what I experienced at Florida, with my name now really becoming a national one. I say that to say this; none of it was normal, especially right away. As I got older, I became more comfortable with the limelight and I learned to adjust. When I was 20 and 21 years old, however, I was, admittedly, stunned by it all.

As I've mentioned before, I was such a big professional prospect that it didn't feel like there was much room for me to be a person. Most people my age at the time were working part-time jobs and wasting their hourly wages at the bar or club. I had to be perfect, all while being everything to everyone, including people who I didn't know.

Each of my steps were followed and counted. Everything I said became a quote. Nobody can prepare for that. Just because a young man is great at football doesn't mean he is great at life yet. Society needs to remember that when constantly praising these kids, then quickly turning on them as soon as they make a mistake. We are setting them up for failure.

I leaned heavily on my family and my agent during all of this. They, along with my faith, were the perfect support system I desperately needed. Though the chatter was at a fever pitch, I mostly felt relatively relaxed entering my pro day. I still did not know where I was going to be drafted, or if I would be drafted at all for that matter, but I felt I had done everything I needed to do. I was in a good place after the chaos of the missed Senior Bowl and the NFL Combine. That is the attitude you want to have when all of the coaches and scouts come to your school to see you and your teammates. Having the "Fab Five" and my entire crew around me on campus was settling. Beyond that, playing football was natural for me at that point. The window dressing was what sometimes bothered me.

That afternoon, I looked good, I felt good and I was glad to see my teammates doing their thing. The uncertainty of the combine had been replaced by the familiar footing of the practice fields at Florida. Out there under that hot sun was where I needed to be.

There were times, though, where things still got crazy for me mentally. I slept on the couch the night before in my apartment as my mother was down and slept in my bed. When I walked in my room, her all-white malteese named Powder was lying directly on my pillow. Both Mama and her dog looked up at me offended as I opened the door. That dog was staring at me like he was a person. That was my lasting impression before I left my crib for the field.

I remember driving to the facility and telling myself to turn it loose today. Our strength coach Rob Glass ran the whole show and told all of us that we earned this opportunity and that nobody was going to disrespect any of us. There was so much encouragement from so many people. My trainer from New Orleans, Tom Shaw, was there. I was busy. I had two private workout sessions, not one, which I didn't even know was allowed.

People kept asking me about my forty yard dash time. Most of the evaluators there were in Tallahassee scouting Florida State the day before. We discussed the 40-yard dash time of one of the Seminole linebackers, Michael Boulware, who remarkably ran somewhere in the 4.3 range. Asked about that, I promptly told everyone that I ran right past him when I played him and that I was a football player. Then I walked away.

After it all, Joel came up to me and said, "The hay is the barn, kick your feet up and relax."

My mama was there the whole time, just as she had always been. Her and that dog Powder. Apparently Jon

Gruden was there, too, though I don't remember him from that event specifically. He later talked with me about him working me out there years later. Coach Gruden somehow remembered all of the details.

The best advice I can give anyone going through the draft process is to be in an environment you trust. To be around people you love. That is why I spent the weeks leading up to the biggest week of my professional life back home in Swainsboro. I wanted to spend time with friends and family, to control what I could control and to keep things simple.

For as busy as we get at times, there still is and always will be value in just taking it all in whenever you can. I tried to, though the anticipation and apprehension was difficult to deal with.

Getting drafted is a monumental occasion, but until you actually get picked, you constantly wonder if you actually ever will. For me, I felt like I was representing so many people beyond just myself. For that reason, there was a persistent fear leading up to the 2004 NFL Draft that often trumped my obvious excitement. While I wanted to get chosen and go to a good situation, I wanted it, in many ways, for everyone else. Though I couldn't control what might happen, I mostly didn't want to let everyone else down.

When I thought about all that was on the horizon, I thought about growing up on a dirt road, my daddy being in jail and my brother being overseas. I thought about all of Swainsboro, Augusta and Gainesville, too. My emotions were all over the place. With my future out in front of me, all I could think about was my past. Mama having to be the backbone. Mama holding it down. Mama leading the way. She was my strength. I wasn't just waiting for a team to draft me, I was waiting for one to pick all of us, me and my mama included.

That responsibility, while awesome, is a big one for a big kid to carry. Even one standing 6'4'', 260 pounds. There were no guidelines to follow. As has been the case my entire life, I just did my best. If it wasn't enough, I was okay with that. I knew there would be a learning curve. I knew there would be mistakes. I also knew that there would be triumphs. Before it all, however, there had to be a phone call.

I spent the draft around loved ones, though I honestly did not know the name of the man who owned the house where we all were. I didn't need a hotel ballroom, simply the home of one of my daddy's friends. Just about everyone who mattered to me was there and that, more than anything else, made it all I could have dreamed of.

In addition to my immediate and extended family, people from various points in my life made it a priority to come to the get-together. My former Butler teammate Isaac West, the greatest athlete I have ever had the pleasure of playing with and someone I have the utmost respect for, drove down with his sister Mya. That gesture meant a lot to me. I was honored to be able to share that time with him. All of the Augusta television stations were on-site.

The pride on the faces of everyone there, some of whom knew nothing about football other than that I played it, was unbelievable. While we didn't know what franchise I would be drafted by or what city I would soon move to, there was a common understanding, even amongst those who had never watched a draft or a game before, that something rare and exciting was happening.

Everybody was telling me congratulations long before my name was ever called. That was one of the unique aspects of that day; I wasn't actually *doing* anything as much as I was just *waiting* for something. I was merely waiting around just like them. To those friends and family, those few hours were a life-changing development. The reality is that the real work had been done years ago. This was a moment a lifetime in the making. Like an out-of-body experience, I was simply watching it all play out.

Before I actually got the call, I had a couple of close calls. To minimize distractions, I didn't use my personal cell phone on draft day, I used the phone of Sister Christine Peeples. Somehow, one of my cousins was still able to dial up that line. When I picked up, not recognizing the number and thinking it was likely a professional team, the voice on the other end of the line yelled out, "What's up 'cuz, you drafted yet?"

That true story was another example of my family at-large. It was all love, just, like a lawn that hasn't been cut in a while, a little rough around the edges.

I still didn't exactly know how all of this was supposed to work. I was kind of expecting a phone call, but I didn't know if it was going to come before or after my name was announced on television. Later in the first round, I really started to pay attention to each pick. Many of the biggest names were already off the board and, though I swear didn't actually think I was going to get drafted until I did, I at least felt like the chances were improving the longer this all went on.

The final pick of the first round belonged to the New England Patriots. As I was watching, Paul Tagliabue stepped to the podium. He looked to his card and said, "With the 32nd pick in the 2004 NFL Draft, the New England Patriots select Ben...". Pause everything. In that moment, I truly thought I was headed to Foxboro. With all of the chatter dramatically fading into the background around me, I slowly started to rise from the couch in a made-for-TV moment, lifting my arms in the air. Suddenly, "...Watson, tight end, Georgia," the commissioner continued. I was happy for Ben, but frustrated that we had the same first name. The news people were fooled, too.

I never thought I would ever be drafted. Before I actually was, though, I thought I had already been.

Not long after that, the phone rang again. It was Tennessee Titans head coach Jeff Fisher. He asked me if I was ready to join the team. I said yes. Coach Fisher put me through to some staffer in logistics. I frame it that way because that is exactly the way it happened.

For all of the attention each NFL Draft gets, you would have thought a choir of singers would have replaced the ringtone, with balloons and confetti falling down like rain. The truth is the call could not have been more regular. Yes, I was ecstatic and nervous and all else in between, but my conversation with Coach Fisher, if you want to call it that, maybe lasted five seconds. There was no enthusiasm in his voice whatsoever. While this may have been one of the biggest days of my life, it was just another work day for Coach Fisher and the Titans.

In a span of mere moments, I was officially in the NFL. I wasn't glowing. I couldn't leap tall buildings in a single bound. I wasn't suddenly a superhero. I was, however, about to be very famous and about to be very rich.

Before all of that, however, I was still just Ben; Troupe, not Watson. I was right down the road from where I grew up in Swainsboro. I was just around the corner from where the town used to have two pools, one for the white people and the other one for everyone else. I was just a glance from where Mama was evicted from her home and Milton Grey, the manager at Citizens Bank, helped her move to an apartment while Daddy was locked up and I was away at college.

More than just the road less traveled, my journey was a path filled with countless relatives and country stores, neighborhood dogs and super roosters and a local mayor who also sold used cars right across the street. All that I had seen and done prepared me for what I was doing and where I was going. As mentioned, I wasn't just heading to Nashville, every single one of us were.

I couldn't stop thinking about the people who paved the way. My parents, my grandparents, my brother, my sisters, my cousins, my aunts, uncles and everyone around me back home all made what was happening possible. Their consistent love and support made the abnormal seem normal. Even those I didn't know as well, neighborhood friends who I saw maybe a few times a year, their smiles and waves gave me motivation.

The haters had their place, too, as I remembered those who said I couldn't while honoring those who always knew that I could. Coaches and teachers, friends and family; it was me who was drafted, but all of us did it together. I wouldn't have wanted to be anywhere but in the

'Boro, the place that groomed me, with the people who molded me.

Thank you Swainsboro. Thank you to my family. Thank God for it all. Thank God for you all.

As I became a professional, regardless of what field it was in, I did so in the shadows of greatness. Well before I joined the Titans, I came from them first.

THE LEAGUE

The great Hugh Douglas once said that the NFL comes with two things: money and memories. He said get as much as you can, as fast as you can. I had a lot of one and will always, if my mind holds up, have a lot of the other. It's actually the latter that I appreciate the most.

I'm not saying it should be this way, but, in the United States of America, playing professional football is about as big as it gets. I often felt it, both the platform and the pressure. Also, the pain. Other times, especially in a huge house full of empty rooms, I felt alone. From the outside looking in, there is a wild mysticism to the NFL and I certainly understand it. Every Sunday is a national showcase. Kids dream about it. Movies magnify it. Almost all of us talk about it. Few, however, live it. Rarely is it what people think.

I am eternally thankful for the opportunity I got to play professional football. I would like to say it's one I earned, though I still can't identify exactly what separated me from dozens of other players at Florida, much less hundreds of others who I competed against overall. It was my greatest honor to line up alongside the best of the best and measure myself in ways I never could have imagined.

Though the NFL was never a fantasy of mine, it became an experience that felt make-believe. Some, after college, go into business, marketing, public relations, accounting or physical therapy; I went right into it all. In no way was I prepared for what I did or saw, nor am I the right person to judge how I performed. That aside, my deepest gratitude goes out to former Tennessee head coach Jeff Fisher and general manager Floyd Reese, who I would later host a radio interview with as we both went on to careers in sports media, for giving me the chance of a lifetime in 2004.

Floyd and I actually visited while working at the 2019 NFL Draft in Nashville, of all places. Again, you just can't make this stuff up.

Back when I got picked in 2004, the NFL Draft was only two days. I was selected on day one. On the second day of the draft, I got onto a Delta plane in Atlanta headed for Nashville. The pilot actually gave me a shoutout over the loud-speaker and the passengers all started clapping. When I stepped onto that jet, I entered a whole new world.

First, the money. It almost feels wrong, given my upbringing and all, to talk so openly about personal finances. But a lot of people still ask me about it and I know everyone thinks about it. That is a big part of the appeal, right? Understand, though, that very few people actually make millions of dollars. The realities of long careers or maximum contracts are unfortunate misconceptions about professional athletes.

For every Peyton Manning, there are one hundred other guys whose combined earnings don't equal his. Everybody is making great money, don't get me wrong, but a decent chunk of NFL rosters feature players who don't last long enough to earn retirement, never have an endorsement deal and aren't even famous in the cities where they play.

Quick, name all of the current fullbacks or primary special teams players you know off of the top of your head. Those guys best represent the average experience. My experience was not average.

Your introduction to the NFL largely depends on where you get drafted. So my experience was top-notch and top-shelf. It was elite. I was welcomed to the pros with open arms.

I was blessed to be selected 40th overall by Tennessee as the Titans' number one pick in 2004. For signing my name on my first professional contract, I made $1.2 million. Think about that. Though I wholeheartedly support initiatives to better educate young players for the fame and fortune that may be coming their way, there is nothing you can do to prepare a 21-year-old for generational wealth. Keep in mind, I was not any smarter than any other kid my age. I wasn't more prepared. I wasn't more mature. I just had more money.

Not that long before I became a millionaire, I was taking nickels, dimes and quarters to the corner store to buy candy. While I was in high school in Augusta, I made $25 a week playing the drums at my church back in Swainsboro. Titus Peeples played the keyboard. The first time I saw myself on the cover of a magazine, I didn't really have the extra money to buy it. A man at the store saw me glance it over and put it back and promptly volunteered to get me a few copies.

When the financial aid department offered to direct deposit my extra scholarship money at Florida, I politely declined because I didn't know what that meant. I had never had a bank account. Forget dollars and cents, all that was coming my way was a different kind of change.

Time and time again, back when this was all new, I would go to an ATM to check my balance and close to one million dollars would be on the receipt. I barely knew how to pronounce all of those numbers, much less process them all. After the shock and awe, the money was simply a magnifier. That's how money works, initially, at least.

The first thing I bought was a brand-new 2004 GMC Yukon. It was literally Titans blue. You could have called it *Smurfs* blue. It had 26-inch gator-scale rims, four 15-inch subwoofers in the back with a sound system and four televisions, including a flip-down screen. I used to play music videos by Nelly in the car.

Did I need all of that? Yes and here is why. Rich or poor, young men do young men things. I had no choice but to scratch that itch. Daddy calls it, "getting that young man up out you".

That money, along with cash I spent on clothes, trips and other cars, obviously could have been put to better use. At one point I actually had five cars and I constantly rotated through many others. Making those ridiculous and unnecessary purchases helped me learn how budgeting worked and helped me better understand the true value of things, though. Honestly, Covenant Partners, aka my financial partners, showed me how money worked. I can still hear Miss Mickie asking me about another car I just bought. They were the absolute best and were the only reason I saved any money.

There is a process to learning how to be an adult, much less doing so as a celebrity with fantasy income. You simply can't fasttrack maturity, though I tried to in my BMW 6 Series and Chevy Camaro 2SS.

Some people buy automobiles to get them from point A to point B. Ultimately, that proved to be the case with me as well. Just in a different way. One of my favorite cars I have ever had was a 1969 Chevelle Malibu with a 454 big block engine in it. It was navy blue, with a light blue interior. I used to drive it to Athlete's Foot in Nashville to look at shoes. As was the case with my rides, I am specific about my shoes. I would go shoe-shopping multiple times a week. It became almost therapeutic for me, a break from the grind. I would get recognized often, though it was refreshing to talk with people about shoes, not just football.

Over time, I developed a nice relationship with one of the salesmen, a genuine, down-to-earth dude. He loved my Malibu, said it was his dream car and talked about it all of the time. With him, I wasn't Ben Troupe, the Titans tight end, I was Ben Troupe, the guy with the '69 Chevelle. After thinking about it, I told him that I would be willing to sell him the car. He was stunned, jumped at the opportunity and we decided on a price. We agreed on a down payment and I trusted him to pay me the rest per month.

A few weeks later, he came to my house to make the deal. As soon as he saw the car in my driveway, he started making wide facial expressions and slowly rubbing his hands together, any man's universal sign of approval. He was so proud of that car, even before it was ever officially his. At that point in my life, the Malibu was one of many things for me. For him, long a goal of his to own this very car, it was everything. It quickly dawned on me, right there in my front yard, the rare position I was in.

When he came back outside with the cash, I stopped him and told him to keep it. I told him that I simply couldn't sell him the car anymore. I gave him that '69 for absolutely nothing, instead. To be able to help somebody and his family, a sales associate who had been so helpful and nice to me for months, was part of me coming of age. Opportunities like those became my everything. I was honored to be playing my part.

That wasn't the first or only time I gave a car away. I gave Gus Scott a watercolor blue 1970s Lincoln Continental convertible with suicide doors and a light blue interior. I gave Darrell Lee a bright green and white 1970s hardtop Chevy Impala with spinners on it. To be honest, I bought those rides for myself. But like Daddy used to say, "you have ten cars, but two feet." I decided to bless two of my boys. Last time I checked, Darrell had painted the Impala all black. Gestures like those were the least I could do for people who had always been there for me.

Each time I gave something away, I felt like I was the one getting something. It really is better to give than to receive.

The money I was paid by the Tennessee Titans, Tampa Bay Buccaneers and Oakland Raiders wasn't just for me, but everybody around me. When an NFL team drafts you, they draft your family and friends, too. It wasn't just my honor to care for those close to me once I was able to, it was my obligation. In Swainsboro and Augusta, I was raised by parents and grandparents and aunts and uncles who always found a way to provide. Now it was my turn.

Though I was barely even a young man, my community was looking up to me; there was no way I was going to look away. I bought Mama a house, bought my siblings cars and paid the bills for countless others. I was thrilled to be able to.

I did what I was supposed to do. I did what was in me to do. I did what I was brought up to do. If given the opportunity, I would do it all again. I wouldn't have been wrong had I not done for my family, but I wouldn't have been right, either. I thought the idea of taking care of friends and family what was everybody did. I was surprised that not everybody in the NFL took care of their people. I guess every situation is unique. Different strokes for different folks.

My money wasn't endless, however. Almost half of it went to the government, my representation then took their cut and, before I bought anybody else anything, I was overwhelmed by my own monthly expenses. Especially after I spent tens of thousands of dollars on my first team dinner in the NFL. Some of the veterans didn't even know my name, they just called me "New Money"as they ordered steak, lobster and liquor. Me picking up the tab continued each week, though future meals were much more affordable.

Every Thursday, which was weigh-in day, our fullback Robert Holcombe would ask me what was for lunch. After I tried to ignore or decline him, he would hit me with the veteran's head shake and I knew that I had to go to Swett's to pick up food for a bunch of the guys. Steve McNair was one of them.

Whether my teammates called me "Ben", "Troupe" or "84", I was simply earning my spot as a rookie by going with Jarrett Payton, the son of the legendary Walter Payton, and Troy Fleming to get those beef tips for the elders.

I had never balanced a budget before, had never financed anything and did not realize how much it cost to be out on your own. While I had a lot of money, I had no idea what to responsibly do with it. And a lot of it was going out of the door as soon as it came in. The one thing about money is that it isn't necessarily about how much you make, but how much you keep. Just because I could buy something didn't mean I needed to. It took me a while to learn that.

It's also worth noting that expensive things are expensive to maintain. One time my battery died in my BMW; it cost $850 for a new one. A freaking battery.

Nobody in my family, nor anyone I had ever personally known, had been wealthy. I was, but I wasn't ready.

I cherished the responsibility God granted me to be there for other people. It did, if I'm being truthful, though, add to the pressure I faced. In addition to being the first draft pick of a professional football franchise and a prominent player expected to start and star right away, I was suddenly a public figure, a businessman, a brand ambassador and a lifeline for dozens of people who helped make me who I was.

I was also just 21 years old. There was no room for any of the anxiety or uncertainty that sometimes accompany being that age.

If I had any doubt on the field, I would have disappointed hundreds of thousands of people, maybe millions. If I had any doubt away from the field, I would have failed the ones who mattered most. A lot of the time it felt like I was barely keeping it all together, smiling and waving and signing autographs while consumed by what-if and what-could-be. What-was was a lot to consider. There were days I was glad to have a helmet to hide my face in. There was nowhere to go but to work.

And work this was. There is at least an aspect of fun and games to the college football experience. The NFL has a straight-forward, tell-you-like-it-is, rip-your-heart-out reality. They don't show you the daily routine because it isn't glamorous. You get there early, you leave late. You watch film, you lift weights. You have one meeting, then head to another. The harshness of the league is serious.

Player contracts aren't guaranteed. They can cut you, regardless of who you are, whenever they feel like it. Even if you have had a ten-year career, they will break all ties with you with a simple slip in your locker. You are supposed to show up, show out and, for the most part, shut up.

I get it, it's a rare opportunity, the money you get paid is obscene and the celebrity that comes with it can turn into eternal fame. But for people who think it is a constant promotional shoot, it isn't. The NFL can be much more of a constant case of the Mondays than the celebrated Sundays everyone sees.

Beyond my personal experiences, I would go on to watch Titans staffers literally lock the best player in franchise history out of the building. Steve McNair tried to return to the facility after being injured and, because of his contract and the possibility that if he got hurt on team grounds the team would be liable, they would not let him in. Workers were holding the door closed as he stood outside. Think about that; the greatest player in Tennessee history, a regular season Co-MVP and a near-winner of the Super Bowl, literally got locked out of the building. I was not prepared for what awaited.

Enter Erron Kinney, the man who saved my career. When I first arrived in Nashville, squinting and wobbling my way through all of the bright lights, he walked up to me, grabbed me, looked me in the eyes and said, "I got you". Beyond him just being one of the tight ends on Tennessee's roster, I knew who Erron was because he played at Florida a few years before me. My first personal meeting with him came right before my introductory press conference with the Titans. His conviction was calming.

There is a presence to Erron, or as I like to call him "E.K." or as Keith Bullock used to call him "Big Smooth", that is deeply reassuring and resolute. Standing 6'7'', he was and remains 275 pounds of raw role model, a long-time philanthropist and accomplished firefighter who has made that civil service his passion. Without E.K., I fail miserably as a professional football player. I desperately needed him. Like Carlos Perez in Gainesville, Erron was my guardian angel in Nashville.

Furthermore, Erron was the greatest teammate that I ever had. Our bond was truly special. My most productive season in the NFL came in year two when I had 55 receptions for Tennessee. Remarkably, Erron had exactly 55 catches for the Titans that season as well. In 2005, Erron, Bo Scaife and I combined for 147 total grabs, one the highest totals for a trio of tight end teammates in pro football history.

What made all of this so powerful is that, at least in theory, I was brought to Tennessee to take Erron's job. I was supposed to be his replacement. Not once, even for a second, did he treat me as a threat. I wasn't anywhere near his standard of excellence anyway. Understand that I was in complete and utter awe of E.K. His professionalism became the model for my career. His perspective became the model for my life.

Erron, explaining every detail and walking me through each step, showed me how to make it in the NFL. He taught me, validated me, inspired me, apologized for me and covered for me. Right away, Erron showed me how to train, how to rest, how to understand a playbook, how to watch film and how to interact with coaches. More importantly, he taught me how to become part of a community when I wasn't yet ready to be and how to be a family man long before I ever would become one. The two main things that Erron showed me were to embrace who I was as a person outside of football and that once I got a family of my own they would become my priority.

I was not capable of following in Erron's footsteps, but I became his shadow nonetheless. Every catch I made should also be part of E.K.'s already impressive totals of 178 receptions for 1,750 yards and ten touchdowns. In my mind, he had at least 284 catches for 2,803 yards and 17 scores.

Erron and his wife Julie opened their arms and opened their home to me. I simply cannot thank them enough. They helped me find balance as a player and a person and gave me the conviction to better handle all that I was dealing with. Both of them helped me continue to cultivate my passion for volunteer work, introducing me to like-minded people in the Nashville area. That family is royalty and they deserve to be treated as such, though they are as gracious and modest as they come.

One of my first experiences with Erron and Julie was when they drove me, early in my rookie season, to a football camp the legendary Steve McNair was hosting. I was happy-go-lucky and didn't know much about the Kinneys yet and was just excited to get to spend some time with "Air McNair". Once we arrived and got out of the car, Steve smiled, his eyes lit up and he gave Erron and Julie a warm embrace. He then coldly and sternly turned to me, didn't say my name, probably didn't even know it and told me to go throw the football with the kids. That is exactly how they, and I, deserved to be treated.

Many of my memories start with the Kinneys. More than the moments of my time in the pros, the people are who and what I remember. There were so many funny stories. E.K. and Julie, like most married couples, wanted to have date nights every now and then. They even asked me to watch their kids once. I am not a good babysitter, especially wasn't then, and I was very much manipulated by their 3-year old Ceanna and 1-year old Elijah. Needless to say, they didn't ask me to babysit again. That said, The Kinneys will always be part of my family.

E.K.,

I want to say thank you, my guy. Thank you for taking me under your wing. Thank you for showing me the difference between being a pro and a professional. You taught me to never cheat the game and always be my best on and, more importantly, off the field. E.K. I do not have an inkling of a career without you. You are my brother for life. I could never say thank you enough. I don't make it in Nashville without you. You, Julie, Ceanna, and Elijah helped me transition and feel at home.

Julie, they don't make 'em like you. The last thing you told me in my very last game at then-LP Field was, "Ben, I'm praying for you". Ceanna, you hustled me at age two and let me know that owning child daycare centers was not in my future. E.K., you were and will always be who I needed and who God sent to help show me the way forward and protect me in this crazy business. E.K., you are a class act. You are the whole truth. To this day, you are the best teammate I ever had the pleasure of playing with and you are also the best all-around tight I've ever played with.

In the words of the great Keith Bullock, you are Big Smooth. Love you Big Smooth. Long live E.K.

Keith Bullock is another one of the leaders I owe my career to. He is one of the top linebackers in NFL history. I once saw him pick off Drew Brees three times on Monday Night Football. I didn't fully know or appreciate it at the time, but Keith was constantly showing me what it took to make it at the next level every single day. There was an unrelenting bar with everything he did. I developed a respect for him that knew no bounds.

Keith officially kept it 100. After blowing up play after play in practice, he once yelled at our offensive coordinator Norm Chow, formerly of Southern California, that, and I'm paraphrasing with gentle editing, he wasn't in the Pac-12 anymore and Keith didn't play for UCLA. He also told Norm that the B.S. he was running in college wasn't going to work here.

Every single thing Keith said, he backed up. Every single one of Keith's expectations, he upheld. Keith was the heart and soul of our team. He used to tell me that everyday was an audition and it was my job to show everyone else that I deserved to be there. At the end of my second year where we went 4-12, Keith stood up after our exit meeting and screamed, "I'm not a loser!"

Keith's mentality, coming with tough love, is what made him special. I never suited up with a better player. "Mr. Monday Night" was Hall of Fame worthy and an even better teammate.

Our locker room was full of grown men. Meaning dozens of guys with wives, children and real-life responsibilities. Just like in college, not all of us were close. There were a few guys, though, who I really enjoyed being around. First and foremost, our tight end rooms were always great. Even after Erron, there was Bo Scaife, who was Vince Young's guy at Texas, Greg Guenther, who went to USC, Casey Cramer, who went to Dartmouth, and future ESPN Radio personality Brian Hartsock out of Ohio State. Like Vince, Ben had a national championship ring. We all saw the bling.

There was also Auburn's Cooper Wallace, who used to make me chuckle with a story of Guss Scott making a play on him in pass coverage and then saying, "you thought you were open...you're a white tight end!" Guys were from all over the place, like Shad Meier who went to Kansas State. I also can't forget Jamie Petrowski, from Indiana State. He brought the laughs and we were actually the only two healthy bodies at tight end for a while in 2006.

Bo Scaife was so much fun to be around and always kept my spirits up. He also loved the Denver Broncos. I'll never forget when we played them, he was walking around on their field starstruck and kept talking about and pointing to "them boys". He was jumping around and bouncing up-and-down when their team was introduced. Especially Denver quarterback Jake Plummer. I had to ask Ben if he was going to be okay and, you know, try to help us win.

Casey Cramer was laid back, even though we picked on him for being an Ivy league guy. He used to try to tell us all how hard it was to play Princeton and Yale. Those efforts were unsuccessful. Casey actually came to my celebrity weekend in Augusta. When he started dancing when the music came on, the entire crowd started chanting, "go white boy, go white boy!"

It was also cool to get to know Ben Hartsock as he was country like me, but was from Ohio. I didn't even know they had places like Swainsboro, Georgia in Ohio. He grew up on a farm and had that farmer's strength to him. Ben looked just like Dennis Quaid. Though he and I became good friends, I didn't like him at first because he had the ability to fill multiple needs on the field. I, unlike Erron Kinney with me, saw him as a threat.

Over time, Ben's perspective really impacted me. He showed me how to be a better teammate and talked openly with me about his struggle to find playing time with Indianapolis. I swear, Ben knew I needed to see my role differently. He helped me find context in competition.

Football is a team sport played by individuals. I had developed an individual mentality and Ben Hartsock helped me rediscover a collective mindset. The greatest thing you can be is a teammate truly supporting your teammates. I became a better football player when I finally realized what being a teammate really meant. The most fun I ever had in the NFL came after my talks with Ben.

I needed Erron Kinney to show me the way. I needed Bo Scaife to keep me loose. And I need Ben Hartock to help me see the bigger picture.

One of the most influential people I ever had the pleasure of being around was another tight end in Ben Hall. My brother-from-another-mother, Ben and I lived together in Nashville and settled into life post-college side -by-side. He was the friend I needed. Ben and I had similar interests, similar experiences and we really hit it off right away. We spent so much time talking about everything outside of football like our goals, our dreams and how to change the world. We were, in thought and in theory, often the same person. In many ways, Ben also helped fine-tune my perspective.

The way Ben Hall carried himself was stabilizing for me. His charisma really helped me continue to find confidence and comfortability in who I was. Going back to my brother Lucus, Titus Peeples and the "Fab Five" at Florida, Ben was another addition to my crew. Every time I saw him, I felt like I was looking in the mirror. Sometimes in life, God does give you a mirror-image of yourself. Mine had my same first name, too. Small-town country boys who both grew up without our fathers, we needed each other at that particular time in our lives.

"B-Hall" and I once ate at Taco Bell for a month-and-a-half straight. We went there so much that the lady in the drive-thru refused to believe that we actually played in the NFL. Amazingly, Ben has since become an acclaimed pastry chef, self-taught, a testament to his brilliance and creativity. His spot "Big Ben's Desserts and Ice Cream" is critically-acclaimed. His place is home to the best banana pudding around and, get ready, a honey bun cake, among other tasty treats. Ben even bakes personalized cakes for the Clemson football seniors every season.

Not long after delivering pancake blocks as a Y tight end, Ben now opts for pastries. He has been serving up the truth for years.

From my fellow tight ends to my quarterbacks, I always appreciated those who were most involved with what I did. Understand this: Steve McNair was as good as anyone to ever do it. The 2003 NFL Co-MVP, his profile was as big as could be when I arrived in Tennessee. I didn't even know how to talk to him. The first time I approached him, I was ready to address him as "Mr. McNair". I may actually have.

Steve had made history before making it to the pros. A Heisman Trophy finalist and the winner of the Walter

Payton Award at Alcorn State, he was selected third over-all in the 1995 NFL Draft as, at that point, the highest-picked African-American quarterback ever. Another example of a superstar coming from Historically Black College and Universities, "Mac" was the consummate franchise pillar. He helped guide and introduce the Tennessee Titans forward after they transitioned from Houston as the Oilers.

Mac was consistent and determined, demanding and steadfast. A true icon of the game, he very nearly, as in a matter of mere inches, led Tennessee to victory in Super Bowl XXXIV. I will never forget Steve's presence. He had an aura to him that resonated and spread like few things I have ever felt. A true superstar quarterback is what this man was.

The news of Mac's death struck me and stopped me back in 2009. It came on, of all days, the 4th of July. I revered this man. For the longest time, he simply called me "Rook". When one of the greatest signal callers of all-time finally called me by my name for the first time, I felt I had arrived. It was so strange for me when we played Baltimore in Nashville and Mac was with the Ravens.

I will always remember the first time I was ever in a huddle with Mac. Once he got the play, he walked right up to me like we were in a movie. He was motioning to me to do something. I was desperately trying to understand what he was wanting as he was physically moving me and patting me on the head. I was so starstruck, I couldn't even function in the moment. All Mac wanted me to do was put my head down so he could see.

Time and time again, Mac would always say, "Let's go play with this little brown ball." He was the truth. I will tell my kids and grandkids about Mac. I miss him.

Rest in peace, Mac, one of the greatest players in NFL history. I can't believe I got to even play with him, much less catch touchdown passes from him.

I watched, with Troy Fleming and Marcus White at my house, as the Titans took another quarterback hero, this time in the 2006 NFL Draft. Tuning into the broadcast as fans, we had no clue which way the organization was leaning leading up to the pick. All of us in the room, though, wanted Vince Young. One of the most amazing college football players ever, Vince immortalized himself with 467 yards of total offense, and a late game-winning 4th down touchdown, in a Rose-Bowl-for-the-ages triumph over USC to win a national championship.

Vince was larger than life. When he was announced as Tennessee's first pick, Troy, Marcus and I jumped off the couch and ran around my living room screaming. It was official: "V.Y. the legend", as we called him, was coming to Music City.

Like Ronald Dowdy at Florida, Vince is full-blown country. Especially at that age, he was a personality all his own. Nashville may be the country music capital of the world, but Vince, from Houston, came to town singing a different kind of tune. Playing with him also introduced me to a different type of athlete as well. Every single one of us who played with Vince had an impersonation of how he talked and acted, though nobody could mimic what he did on the field. I will also tell my kids and grandkids about Vince.

Marcus White, like Ben Hall, was a combination of many of my friends. He kept it 100 like Keith Bullock, kept it light like Bo Scaife and kept it country like Vince Young and Ben Hartsock. He didn't patronize anyone. Marcus also introduced me to Meco Isadore, who was like Ashely Moore was for me at Florida.

Interestingly enough, I met Meco's daughter Yamese first, seeing her at Marcus' house. I asked everyone who the "little mixed girl" was. Meco came into the room, shocked and offended. Not the best way to introduce myself. I made a fool of the moment, saying that her daddy had to be white. Troy Fleming argued that she was completely black because of her hair. Meco clarified things, explaining that her father was indeed a black man.

From there, I kept inappropriately joking that Yamese's daddy was the milkman. Despite that unique introduction, Meco, who went to Auburn with my high school teammate Carlos Rogers, and I became great friends. She remains a close, personal confidante and has been like a sister to me for years. I am so proud of the work we have done together as she and I have partnered on a children's book series, *Judee and Jon*, which tells stories from the perspectives of young black and brown children. She is yet another example of my growth. I talk to Meco everyday.

Meco,

When I first met you, let's just say that you didn't agree with my assessment on who Yamese's daddy was! LOL! Meco, you are a dreamer who I needed to show me how to dream past football. We both shared a love for football; you and your Auburn Tigers and me and my Florida Gators. We became friends. We became family. We are family.

The conversations we had, how we talked about life, our faith and how we were going to go into business together...it was the start of something special. The fact that we are published authors and you are the reason for it is a testament to your greatness. I'm grateful for you, your prayers, your friendship and your encouragement. Never change, Meco. Abram and Yamese are blessed to have you as a mother. I'm blessed to have you as a sister.

While I was in the NFL, It was incredible the people that I met. Future Hall of Fame center Kevin Mawae, born just down the road from me in Savannah, Georgia, helped me further understand why the little things were such a big deal. He didn't speak a lot, but when he did, everyone made sure and listened.

Kyle Vanden Bosch, from Nebraska, was a white dude with a completely bald head who wore red contacts. I enjoyed being around him, but always felt he was a tiny bit crazy. I mostly just smiled at him and walked away. Albert Haynesworth, for his reputation, was really a nice guy. I also thought Adam "Pac-Man" Jones was misunderstood. Pac was one of the most gifted athletes I ever played with. I am super proud of the career he had.

You had fellas bring some West Coast style to the south, Drew Bennett from UCLA and LenDale White from USC. There was the inspirational story of the late Todd Williams, who grew up homeless, Cortland Finnegan with his little red mohawk and the unmistakable swagger of Samari Rolle. NFL locker rooms are full of eccentric and weird people. I mean that with all of the love in the world.

My first extended introduction to a teammate, however, was with a cool, down-to-earth guy who remains an important friend of mine in Troy Fleming. I actually heard him get drafted while I was at the Titans facility. I also got into a staring match with him when we first met.

Troy and I were rookie roommates, which was a great experience for me. A fullback out of Tennessee, Troy actually finished his career with the second-most rushing yards in high school football history with 9,442 at nearby Battle Ground Academy in Franklin. Herschel Walker rushed for 3,167 yards his senior year of high school; you could have given him a second senior season with that exact same production and he still wouldn't have matched Troy's prep total.

I was fortunate to be paired off with such a standup person. Being around Troy had a positive impact on me and he, too, is an unquestioned part of who I am.

When Troy and I arrived at the Millennium Maxwell House Hotel in Nashville, we actually walked in on each other in the same room. We had an uncomfortable brief glaring session, a couple of heated who-are-you exchanges and then promptly became great friends for life. Troy was the strongest football player I ever played with. He could have run that rock more had we needed it, too.

Me, Ben Hall and Jabril Wilson all went to Troy's wedding. It took Jabril like an hour-and-a-half to come downstairs for us to actually leave. On a serious note, Troy made it a point to make sure that I was there to see he and his wife exchange vows. That is how you can tell someone is important to you, that they want you to be part of the biggest moments of their life. One-time roommates, Troy and I are brothers forever.

Two administrators were especially-important to me finding my way in Tennessee. There was Tina Tuggle, who worked in player development, who was always there for me to talk to. She never made me feel like a player or an employee and always treated me as a person. I needed relationships like those in the building, even if she was working upstairs. Marcus Robertson, a former standout on Tennessee's Super Bowl team, was another person I looked to for guidance in the player development department. He gave me real talk when I needed it and could relate to me as he knew what it was like being a professional player.

In what proved to be an important revelation, Marcus was quick to continue to show me that my influence went well beyond the field. Just like Ron Zook revealed to me the importance of community service at Florida, Marcus added another chapter to that story of mine in Tennessee. In terms of life after football, he also helped me develop a personal brand.

My time with the Titans was terrific. After going 4-12 and 5-11 my first two years, we started to put it all together in 2006. In 2007, we made the playoffs. I was never an All-Pro, never a Pro Bowler, but I started a game in the postseason. Beyond just being part of a highlight-reel scene in San Diego, Arnold Schwarzenegger was on the sidelines, I was competing at the NFL's highest level. That was the pinnacle of my career and an achievement I remain so proud of. I competed against players like Philip Rivers, LaDanian Tomlinson and Antonio Gates. I was there.

What a day it was, even though we didn't pull it out. I will always remember that matchup and Antonio Cromartie even gave me a little something extra to take back with me. He hit me so hard, my lip swelled up like Professor Klump's. I was the comedy relief for the team as we flew back home after losing to the Chargers. Looking back, I still think we should have won that game. Our defense held San Diego to 17 points. Somehow, I led the team with three catches and 44 yards.

I still love the city of Nashville and was honored to get to cover the 2019 NFL Draft there as a credentialed member of the media. Everything about the downtown scene, from the fans to the festivities, was awesome. My teammates were so good to me in Tennessee. A number of them took part in community events with me. Some, like Vince Young, LenDale White, Randy Starks, Pac-Man Jones, my tight end brothers and others, even came with me to a fundraiser I hosted in Augusta.

The Nashville community was great to me as well. That southern hospitality is what I'm all about. Home to my first actual house, Nashville will always feel like home.

Most of what I experienced in the NFL meant more to me as I got older. I didn't quite realize all that I was doing in the moment as I was just trying to make it day by day. In my time in Tampa, I was constantly engulfed by Jon Gruden's enthusiasm. I wasn't ready for Coach Gruden all day, every day. He would add the word "man" after every time he said my name and would talk about me to my face as if I wasn't there: "Ben Troupe, man, he's a football player, man."

Coach Gruden gushed about me and talked of how big of a fan he had been of me since college, recalling previous interactions with me that I didn't even remember. In a truly unique way, Coach Gruden's personality was fun, strange and exhausting all at once. There is nobody quite like him.

This cannot be emphasized too much: Jon Gruden loves football. He loves calling plays and he loves watching people win with them. Coach Gruden would always tell me things like, "I'll call a play for you, man, you will score and I'll get the credit," or, "We'll win a Super Bowl, you might get a commercial, but I'll get a street named after me, man." He had constant parallels he used, like telling me that I was a boxer and that he was my trainer. I would laugh when Coach Gruden would say things like, "Knock on wood if you're with me, men," or, "Santa Claus is coming, man."

This is a coach who was a master motivator. That has keyed a lot of his professional success. Coach Gruden was and remains a sound-bite guru: "Everyone has a dream, man, but we're gonna be their nightmare." His mindset was constant and relentless. One time we were at a bowling alley and he just walked up to me and said, "You've got a lot of talent, man."

It's like we were in a movie and he was constantly in character playing himself. Sometimes I wasn't really sure who he was talking to. He had a script he was following, for sure. Coach Gruden let me know that you had to deeply care about football, man.

I will always remember the fact that Coach Gruden was the first person who called my phone when I initially became a free agent. That meant a lot to me. It's humbling to think about. Coach Gruden not only constantly reminded me that he personally scouted me at my pro day at Florida, but that he was really interested in me then.

Looking back, I watched the incomparable Hall of Famer Derrick Brooks take his hard hat to work everyday and leave absolutely no doubt. Keith Bullock, in my opinion, is the best weak-side linebacker ever. Derrick is the greatest ever and it's not even close. He made the most of every single opportunity on the practice field. I knew it was the beginning of the end for him when, for the first time ever, I saw him motion to another linebacker to replace him in our game against New Orleans.

Simply being around Derrick made me better at everything I did, on the field and off. One of the great moments in my career came when he complimented my route-running and talked about my body control and leverage. That meant so much to me.

I will always remember Derrick for being a businessman, a community man and a family man. He even helped start a school in the Tampa area, Brooks Debartolo Collegiate High School. I will always respect Derrick for being a pro's pro. In 2018, I saw him on the sidelines next to his son DeCalon, a linebacker like his dad, while covering the Florida State-Virginia Tech game. Seeing them together was special.

Additionally, I was inspired by the story and selflessness of Warrick Dunn. He is one of the great philanthropists this country has ever seen, buying and building houses for needy families. We sometimes throw the word "hero" around a lot, but Warrick truly is one. His book *Running For My Life, My Journey in the Game of Football and Beyond*, where he talked about the murder of his mother, who was a police officer, was the first one I ever read. It was life-changing.

I even bought my first laptop from Warrick, though I think he ripped me off. Our lockers were right next to one another. That wasn't the case initially, but Warrick hated that Chris Hovan always left wet clothes and towels on the floor, so his locker got moved near mine. I'm thankful for that.

Derrick Brooks and Warrick Dunn were both superstar players, but I will think of them more for what they did away from the game. Both men are legends.

My time in Tampa was special. People sometimes think their legacies center on what others think of them. Though I played in just two games with the Buccaneers before suffering a plantar fasciitis injury that led to a neverending heel bruise, I'm proud of my time in Tampa. I knew that I could still compete. I earned the respect of Derrick Brooks and Warrick Dunn, Ronde Barber and Jon

Gruden. I enjoyed interacting with players like Chris Hovan, Jeff Garcia, John Gilmore, Dexter Jackson, Alex Smith and Jerramy Stevens, who would go on to marry U.S. Women's National Team soccer star Hope Solo.

One guy in particular who made Tampa what it was for me, similar to Erron Kinney and Ben Hall in Tennessee, was another tight end in Daniel Fells. Number one, he was strong as an ox and could lift anything in the weight room. We were similar in that we learned about each other through each other. When I moved out of the hotel I was in, I stayed with Daniel until I found my own spot. He went to UC Davis and taught me about and helped me embrace West Coast culture and style like the hyphy movement and E-40, aka 40 Water. Daniel could also cook his behind off and didn't want anybody else in the kitchen when he was. I'm surprised he doesn't have his own restaurant like Ben Hall.

Tampa wouldn't have been Tampa without Daniel. God, again, knew who I needed. He sent me Daniel. I am forever indebted to Him and him.

Just like in Tennessee, my time in Tampa helped me further my passion for volunteer work. I will always cherish my experiences speaking to schools and learning how to become more civically involved while I was down there. Living in that area helped continue to cultivate my love for people. All that I was capable of was starting to finally sink in. In reality, Tampa was the final piece for me as I was a complete asset for the team. I was a true pro and I constantly gave my all. I wasn't "stealing" as guys sometimes say when players aren't always full-go.

My last live snaps in the NFL happened with the Buccaneers in 2008. Fittingly, they came against my home-state Atlanta Falcons.

In Oakland, I saw the unique life and times of a young Lane Kiffin. When he was hired at only 33 years old, very few people on the team, some of whom were actually older than him, respected him. The Raiders put him in a bad situation. I like Lane a lot, but he wasn't ready for what he stepped into. I even felt bad for him. He is a good coach with an innovative style and an understanding he learned from his father Monte, a long-time NFL assistant and the inventor of the famed "Tampa Two" defense. He was the defensive coordinator when I was with the Buccaneers. Derrick Brooks used to make that thing work.

The elder Coach Kiffin used to tell me to take it easy on his defenses. It was remarkable to me that I got coached by the father and then hired by the son. That time and place was not the right time or place for Lane. The struggles, however, probably made him better in the long run.

I also still feel bad for the fans in the Bay. Oakland is where the Raiders belong and "Raider Nation", which is a very real thing, has the most passionate group of fans I have ever been around. They are the most dedicated fans in the NFL. We played in Miami, over 3,000 miles away, and there was silver and black everywhere. I was a no-body at that point in my career, but people still recognized me everywhere because of the team I was with.

The Colosseum, dirt on the field and everything, was electric. I wasn't with the organization long, but I understood what that franchise meant to that community. I also appreciated the history of where I was. It was amazing to talk with all-time greats like Dave Casper and Kenny Stabler. Guys from the franchise's glory days were always so gracious. I have gotten to do radio shows in the Savannah area with Raiders icon George Atkinson, a Georgia-native who went to an HBCU in Morris Brown.

The closest I ever got to the late Al Davis, the iconic former owner of the team, was when he walked by me in the hallway once. He was a god to people.

Even though I was barely in the Bay, I remember many teammates there, too. Nnamdi Asomugha, married to the actress Carrie Washington, was a first-team All-Pro corner. In 2008, he might as well have been Deion Sanders. Receivers would come up to him before games and honestly ask him to take it easy on them. He and DeAngelo Hall were a great corner tandem. I played with college football legend Darren McFadden, who always talked about his home state of Arkansas. He represented the Natural State. We represented the SEC out west.

Oakland, on a personal level, let me know that I could make it outside of my comfort zone. I had spent my entire life in the South up until that point. I was able to thrive on the West Coast, though my flight from Atlanta was the longest one I had ever been on by far. It was different, but I found a way to fit in. I had always lived within driving distance of my family, which was obviously not the case in California. There were some trying times, but my life wouldn't be as complete without those experiences. I was finally a grown up. Not by choice, but by circumstance.

My career came full-circle in about a week leading me to Oakland. I played in my last game with the Buccaneers against the Falcons on Sunday, September 14 of 2008. I came in and watched the game film on Monday. I got cut, getting first notified by a phone call from my brother, who saw it on the news, on Tuesday. I flew to Atlanta on Wednesday and tried out for the Falcons on Thursday. One of the staffers working me out was my former Florida teammate Ran Carthon, who was a scout. That same night, I flew to Oakland. I tried out for the Raiders on Friday and made the team.

Al Davis pointed to me from his box and literally gave me a thumb's up. Like he was a Roman king or something. From there, I left with the team for Oakland's game at Buffalo. Outside of former Florida star Gerard Warren, who always called me "Benjamin", I didn't personally know anyone on the team.

In a span of five days, I had flown over 8,200 miles. I was tired. That, ladies and gentleman, is the business of the league.

Nothing about the NFL is normal. I didn't want my experience to be, either. My goals, once I accepted the fact that professional football was actually happening, was that I wanted to be the first player from Florida drafted in 2004, I wanted to be the first prospect taken by the team I went to, I wanted to play multiple years at the next level and I wanted to go out on my own terms. With God's grace, I accomplished all of that.

Injuries limited what I was able to do in Tampa and Oakland, but I still had opportunities when I finally called it quits; Arizona, Atlanta and the New York Giants, to name a few. I turned down the chance to come back for another season. I felt like I had earned the right to tell a professional football team, "No, thank you." All along, I wanted to ask where the door was and not be shown the exit. I walked away knowing that I had more I could have done, knowing that I had more to offer. Truthfully, I'm really proud of that.

I understand that some guys retire with a desire to come back and play more. Not once did I ever regret my decision to hang up my cleats when I did.

I think about that a lot, the fact that I had Arizona Head Coach Ken Whisenhunt, Pass Game Coordinator Matt Miller, Run Game Coordinator Russ Grimm and General Manager Rod Graves all out on the field with me as I tried out. After I showered, President Michael Bidwell came up to me and said that he had already talked to Joel Segal and they had a contract ready for me to sign. I told him no. I told them all no.

Fascinatingly, the coach I turned down to end my career was an Augusta-native in Whisenhunt. Again, you can't make this stuff up.

Understand that I didn't head west with that mindset. I had some time after my workout to think about my future and I decided that the fact that they wanted me so badly was ultimately the affirmation I needed to step away. The Cardinals coaches and administrators couldn't understand my decision, but it felt right in my heart and soul. I always wanted to walk away on my own terms and I was able to do just that.

While I was not ready for the start of my career, I was ready for it all to be done. Now older, I look back and smile.

I played in the golden era of safeties, hybrid defenders who most often matched up with me in coverage. Among others, I went head-to-head with superstars like Brian Dawkins, John Lynch, Troy Polamalu, Ed Reed, Bob Sanders, the late Sean Taylor and Tank Williams. I am proud to have gone up against those guys.

Troy, who never said anything at all on the field, came up to me once holding my towel and politely said, "I think this is dirty, you may want to get a new one." I caught the first touchdown of the 2005 NFL season against Troy and the last touchdown of my career against Brian. "Dawk" hit me in my chin so hard one time that I couldn't feel my face for the remainder of the game. Ed once complimented me on a fake punt I ran that was called back due to penalty.

The memories are many. Few were better than beating the Packers in Green Bay on Monday Night Football. We shut Lambeau Field down. Ray Lewis used to always address me by name, which I thought was interesting. He would say things like, "Ben Troupe, we're gonna play some football out here today." I always expected him to be like 6'8'', 280 pounds, but he was barely six feet tall. He would light you up, though.

I got to play on the same field as the one-and-only Deion Sanders when he was wearing number 37 with Baltimore. He was still Prime, a true celebrity. In addition to watching Peyton Manning do his thing from the sidelines, I can't forget the entire Indianapolis defense talking non-stop trash every time we played them. Same with the Jaguars, at least when they were good.

There were really tough moments, too. The late Marquis Cooper sadly drowned while we were both with the Raiders. His accident occurred in Clearwater not far from where I lived. At first, certain people even thought it was me given the Florida-Oakland connection. Another teammate of mine, Damien Nash, died while I was with Tennessee. The shock, both times, was similar to what I experienced at Florida with the passing of Eraste Autin. I remember talking with Javon Walker about how his former Denver teammate Darrent Williams was killed. These tragedies hit the NFL community hard.

I will always remember my teammates and those I competed against. Especially guys from south and east Georgia. Even now, I still think about leaping over Folkston's Champ Bailey, which essentially became my calling card as a player. The fans, even going back to my days in college, liked when I jumped over defenders. Honestly, I was just trying not to get squared up on or embarrassed. Thank God it all worked out.

Despite my best efforts, I simply cannot put into words how grateful I am to have played in the NFL. It came with life-altering money for me and my family. It continues to open doors for me in ways that I never could have imagined. The experiences I had forced me to mature. There is no education you can buy for all that I learned.

Gratitude expressed and unending, there were aspects of the league that simply weren't for me. The wear and tear on my body, for one. Playing professional football hurts. I hurt then and I hurt now. Some of what I have felt physically and mentally, for years, scares me. I have nightmares. I get depressed. I get headaches. I get angry. I can't remember things. Especially with the news that has come out since I quit playing, I now know those manifestations are from my time in the NFL.

Honestly, I worry about what more may be to come. I was part of the class-action lawsuit against the league and continue to be evaluated by doctors of different types for a long list of symptoms that I now have. I always knew there was an inherent risk to playing football, but I did not know the full scope of what that risk truly was. I'm not sure that information was always completely presented to me.

The mad rush of the NFL was also tiring. There is such a constant sense of urgency, so much pressure to win, certainly, but also to meticulously train every fiber of your body and mind. It was hard to keep up. I was physically and mentally exhausted. To simply maintain yourself as a viable option on the ultimate field of competition, you have to be 100%-in every day.

Football, in the end, was no longer fun to me. While it was my job, I never wanted it to feel like a job. I knew it was work, but when it felt like work I knew something had to be done. I never fell out of love with the game as football will always be a defining part of who I am, but I did fall out of love with the process. I was tired of checking my emotions at the door.

I needed a break and, in the NFL, there isn't one unless you completely sever the tie. I loved to compete, still do, but once the game has left your mind it's time to get out of the way.

Admittedly, I also didn't necessarily enjoy the limelight. I was always grateful to the fans and still am honored to sign autographs and take pictures, but I felt like playing in the NFL put me on a pedestal. I was uncomfortable with that. I consider myself to be just like everyone else and I live and carry myself that way. Sometimes, I got the vibe that such an attitude wasn't always good enough at that level.

Even with the money that came with it, I couldn't fake my way through everything that I did. I'm Ben Troupe from Swainsboro, Georgia and, to be straightforward, anything more than that was always a little much for me. That doesn't mean that I don't embrace success as I absolutely do. I constantly chase it. What I do not vouch for, however, is the notion that what I do makes me better than anyone else. I can't walk that walk and won't talk that talk.

To be frank, I needed more. I had lived the NFL life, but was ready to pursue other options and be known for other things. One of the toughest aspects of being a football star is that it can limit you from being much else. At least that was the case for me. I was a tight end at the game's highest level. I was ready, though, to move on to the next phase of my life. I didn't feel I could do that and be a professional football player all at once.

The great Herm Edwards once said that football isn't a career, it's an opportunity. Would I do it all over again? Of course. In a heartbeat. That said, I never once thought about turning back around. The future remains my focus.

After years of running downfield, my direction still remains forward.

MY ROCK

The ladder I have climbed throughout my life has been held firmly in place by a bold and powerful woman. Strong and steadfast, my mother hasn't always been seen or been heard, but every step I have taken has been made with her out in front. I, even as a fully grown man with children of my own, continue to hold her hand as she shows me the way. I am honored and grateful to be able to follow in her footsteps.

Always there for whatever I need, Mama is my shelter from the cold, my water when I'm thirsty and my plate of pork chops when I'm hungry. Mama is my best friend. She is my biggest supporter. She is also my biggest critic. She is there to pump me up and there to calm me down. She is there to offer her perspective, even when I don't ask for it. Each of those roles are equally important.

People sometimes talk to me about how my mama asks a lot of questions. That she may listen to respond, not to understand. Make no mistake about it, Mama is proud in her beliefs and eager to share them. She has quite the story to tell, too. Mama will tell you the truth because she has lived it. She is it.

With all that my mama has seen, she still looks back with comforting eyes. Even when there is a disagreement. Even when an argument arises. Even when she or I get frustrated. There is a constant grace that follows Mama's every move, a warm, assuring glimmer. I will always bask in that glow. I will always be a reflection of that shine. My mama lights my way.

While my father's life has come with lessons, my mother always made sure I had the stability to understand them. Without her, I don't make it. And I'm not just talking about making it to the University of Florida or the NFL.

Growing up, there were honestly times where I downright hated my daddy. Hated him, or at least thought I did. I didn't know who he was. I didn't know what he was doing. I didn't know where he was. I certainly knew where he wasn't. Through it all, as a young boy, a teenager and a young man, I wasn't sure how he felt about me. As a child, I was always told there was a difference in how you feel and what is real. As a teenager, I was struggling with all of that.

Though I understand his journey more now, and have a deep and genuine respect for all that he suffered through and ultimately overcame, Daddy's absence meant that Mama had to be two parents in one. She, dealing with more than my siblings and I will ever know, had to find a way when there was no way to find one. She was our entire family when there wasn't much other family around.

There are few heroes in life more selfless and valiant than a single mother, especially when that unfathomable responsibility comes with four children, a new and unknown community and the uncertainty of a husband crippled by addiction and incarceration. I understand what NBA great Kevin Durant meant when he said his mother was the real MVP. Anything that my siblings and I were able to accomplish was a direct result of Mama's constant support and fierce advocacy.

Mama's faith is and has been the foundation for our family. Her fearlessness got us through the most trying of times.

My mother has always, without hesitation, put us first. She once told us that it was her job to give up her goals for the betterment of our lives if need be and that nobody else, outside of her or our grandmother, would raise us no matter what. That reality wasn't her trying to make an excuse, rather her letting us know how and why life was unfolding the way that it was. Powerfully, it was Mama telling us to trust her and believe her when she was telling us that everything was going to be okay.

Even at a relatively young age, I found so much security in that promise. Through all that my father put her through, Mama stood tall, and stood by him, regardless of the overwhelming tally that all of that adversity took. She bent, but never broke. She cried, but never quit. She rested, but never folded. She walked by unwavering faith when everyone else's stopped and trembled.

Not once, in all of this, did Mama ever tell me or my siblings what we couldn't be or what we couldn't do. She was a constant and encouraging reminder of all that was possible and all that was good.

Understand this; Mama never once settled. It would obviously have been understandable if she, feeling absolutely beat down, stayed in her hometown, continued to lean heavily on extended family as we always had and played it safe, for lack of a better phrase. With all of the chaos that was engulfing all of us and her, most specifically, she still somehow pushed on. She absolutely did not accept the circumstances that life was giving her.

The reason we left the comfort and familiarity of Swainsboro for the risk that was Augusta in the mid 1990s was because our mother was chasing opportunity. She wanted more, not for herself, but for her family. A bigger city offered the chance at that. We moved to Augusta so that Mama could attend Augusta State University, her individual pursuit of education serving as our collective way forward.

In addition to raising four children and striving to provide us all with the best life possible, Mama added this extra responsibility to set a real life example for Lucus, Nikki, Carianna and I. She was still setting an example for her husband and our father, too. That is leadership. On the sometimes-mean streets of Augusta, Mama was showing all of us that you always keep fighting for your family.

People have asked me how I found ways to break tackles, run past defenders or jump over people in football games. I had been watching Cheryl Troupe do it on the field of life for years.

My mother remains an inspiring mix of grit and grace. Her mental strength is something that always amazes me because she is standing the test of time. She is how I know I'm built to last. She is built to last. Nothing has knocked Mama down.

Our family, during the height of my father's struggles, could have very easily and very understandably fallen completely apart. We all could have been left to our own devices, with the most extreme of consequences potentially a possibility. Aside from keeping us safe and focused, how Mama managed the utter fear of not knowing where Daddy was or what he was doing, is beyond me.

There were stretches wehn she didn't even know if he was alive or not.

For the longest time, this woman shouldered that burden alone. It wasn't until I was older that I even fully understood all that my father was into. I obviously had questions when he would disappear for days at a time, but, growing up, you always trust your parents and assume the best when giving them the benefit of the doubt. I fought off reality as long as I could.

Somehow, Mama sheltered us from all of that worry the best she could. Somehow, she kept her poise and maintained an environment where even her older children couldn't sense the full extent of danger around, much less her true emotions.

Mama found enough money to pay our bills, found extra time to better herself for our sake, kept her kids on the straight and narrow and did so in the face of staggering adversity. Her experiences would have crippled the average person; nothing about my mama, however, is average.

To this day, she carries herself with her head held high, a humble and thankful smile on her face and no outward battle scars from the wars she has fought. Battle-tested, yes, battles both won and lost. Mama has remained a fierce soldier through it all. Angels walk through mountains and valleys that way. My mama may have been going through hell, but she kept going and never once lost faith.

Mama made Augusta work for our family with sheer fortitude and persistence. Walking shoes, dress shoes or slippers, she always laced up her work boots early each morning. She built a future with her heart and her hands. She did so tirelessly. She never asked for praise along the way, just the opportunity to offer it to the Almighty. Tall and stoic, Mama is the strongest person in the world to me.

What is amazing is that my mother didn't just raise Lucus, Nikki, Carianna and I, but, for years at a time, she raised our daddy as well. Directly and indirectly, Mama helped John Troupe find himself, find his faith and find his family once again after he was lost in the wild and wilderness. Daddy had to be born again, for sure, but our mother played the leading role in that re-raising. She taught each and every one of us the importance of compassion, forgiveness and unconditional love. She did so without ever having to explain it.

Those examples continue to be taught and learned everyday, with Daddy now thriving as an ambassador of similar means. It was Mama who pulled him through. For years, this was a man who ran the streets searching for drugs. His wife proved to be the heroine he truly needed.

When citing miracles and uplifting acts of kindness, people understandably offer the phrase "look at God". I've done that by looking at the same beautiful face for years. I see love in Mama's eyes and feel affirmation in her smile. A glance at her is a lifetime look at Daddy's trials and tribulations. Mama is the before and the after.

With a stubborn nature, my mama believes that if you just do what she tells you to do, you will be moving in the right direction. And for good reason. One day at my Aunt Tutta's house, my cousin Lil' Robert and I were having a conversation. While most of my extended family there wanted to talk football with me, which was great, Lil' Robert came up and said something truly profound about Mama. He said to me, "You know why you have been so successful, right?...because of Aunt Cheryl."

Lil' Robert explained to me that my mother had the Midas Touch, meaning everything she touches turns to gold. Mama is a prayer warrior and the answers to those prayers can clearly be seen. Prayer changes things. Her faith and fellowship led to all of her kids being successful. Everyone in our extended family has benefited from her touch. One time in church, a pastor told my mother exactly that; that she had the golden touch. People were coming up and reaching out to her at the service.

My mama, through prayer, led me to Florida. She prepared me to be successful in Augusta, Gainesville, Nashville and beyond. Everything I accomplished, she felt in her heart and soul years before. Not one day goes by without my mother praying for all of us in the family. She inspires everyone around her. We continue to follow that example, thankful and uplifted.

On vacation in Virginia Beach one year, Daddy was talking to the entire family about what he was thankful for. He explained to me that, growing up, he prayed that he would go to college, be in the military and become a professional athlete. Though he didn't accomplish all of those goals himself, his children did. Mama made it possible for all of those dreams to come true. She willed us across the finish line, races we are still running. She is constantly creating a new beginning, all with the same tried and true approach.

My mama is a character because all she does now is go to church, watch TV and talk about how poorly behaved some of the children are at the schools where she works. She is unique because she keeps a very small circle: her church, her children, her grandchildren and, her best friend, her imagination. She is also always ready to talk.

I cannot stress this enough: my mama cannot wait to tell you what she thinks before you even get done saying to her what is actually on your mind. I'm not saying she isn't understanding, but Mama is built to respond. She cannot help it and she isn't trying to help it, either. If my mama doesn't react to something I say to her, that means she didn't hear me right.

With all of that said, I learned from my mother that, even in times when it is completely natural and justifiable to look down on people, it's our charge to look up to the heavens. All of us are imperfect creatures, lacking the discipline to make the most of all of the gifts we have received. To judge others is to also judge ourselves. There simply aren't enough courtrooms in the country for that long of a hearing.

Mama believes in forgiveness, believes in reconciliation and, know this, not just regarding my father. I have failed my mother, given her reason to be disappointed and question my judgment. Every time, she has offered her opinion of my missteps, sure, but also her unwavering love and support. Imagine if we all lived life that very same way? The only thing holding us back is our own pride and bitterness.

This is a woman who empowers people. Make no mistake about it, though, she does so in her own way. Mama doesn't want any assistance. She believes she can do it all. She does so at her church and in the community, with her actions and with her thoughts. After all, Mama is a teacher, one who found a way to earn her college degree while providing for her family at the same time. And no matter what or who she complains about, she loves all of the kids she teaches.

Well before I experienced the firsthand benefit of philanthropic work at Florida, I saw it at home. A seed was planted and we all know the power that a tiny mustard seed can have when it is tied to faith.

It says in the Bible that nothing new happens under the sun. Every time I lend a helping hand, I show up at a civic event or I have the honor of speaking to people in need of a positive message, I feel my mother's influence. I channel her passion for service. People say that I have my daddy's eyes. I have my mama's vision. He does now, too. I cannot explain how satisfying it is that all of our various paths have led to a collective common cause. God does, in fact, bless the broken road.

The fruits of my mama's labor are clear to see. For all of my insecurities, I have been able to realize every goal I have ever set for myself. Beyond just playing college football and reaching the NFL, I have been able to become a traveled motivational speaker, develop a secondary career in sports media and be, I hope and pray, an extension of the good that my mama has so long been.

Lucus is a real, live American hero. His efforts in North Africa and the Middle East helped make the world a better, safer place. Never did Lucus let his concern for his own personal well-being outweigh his concern for the mission or his men. Just like our mother, he sacrificed his safety and sovereignty for the betterment of others. Nikki, following perhaps most-directly in Mama's footsteps, is a certified social worker who has been there for families in tough times in medical facilities all across the state. She remains a constant advocate for those in need, much like the woman she looks so much like. Carianna, our baby sister, has Mama's same persistence and passion for family. Our youngest couldn't have a better standard to strive for. None of us could.

Just as Mama was there for the four of us, she has that same unconditional love for her grandchildren as well. The more things change, the more they stay the same. Our mother is, without question, this family's rock. We have all leaned on it from time to time.

I make it a point to talk to my mama every single day. We have always been close. Sometimes a little too close. There was an instance when I was at Florida where she didn't hear from me for 24 hours so she promptly called the campus police and told them that I was missing. Kindly, they took her concerns in stride and reminded her that I was a college student out on my own for the first time and just might have been a little bit distracted. That is how tight we are and have always been.

Even as I settle into middle-age, Mama remains a resource that I need. We talk family and religion, news and sports; her constant regard for the late Kobe Bryant being one of the two of three best basketball players ever remains a regular talking point that we dive into and discuss. I take her advice, from topics ranging from my career to my personal life and I do so because I solicit it. I don't necessarily always agree with Mama, but there is wisdom and love in her perspective. What could possibly be more valuable than that?

We have all heard of siblings or best friends or couples, mainly, who can literally finish each other's sentences. Mama and I are that way. In the past, teammates or co-workers have asked me about my relationship with her as they hear us on the phone constantly. Instead of trying to explain it to them, I offer a real-time display of our shared symmetry for their entertainment. Any series of questions I ask Mama, I can quote verbatim, ahead of time, what her exact response will be. People always look at me crazy when I tell them this. They then look at me even crazier when it actually happens.

Think Mike Lowrey whisper-quoting Marcus Burnett in the *Bad Boys* movies. I can do that, with any topic, with my mama. I wouldn't be the same person if I couldn't. It's not merely that I have memorized what she says, I have studied how she thinks. If I am that close to her perspective, I am most certainly on the right track.

Like me, Mama can mold herself to any moment without ever compromising who or what she is. A country girl who got married very young, she will forever be sandals on an old dirt road, eating cornbread after church and yelling at the kids to stop playing in her house and to get outside. This woman can also bring any room, in any fancy dining hall or big city, to a complete stop with her beauty and radiance, often on display in a long, flowing dress with her hair worn up high like a crown.

As a teacher, Mama will make it a point to stand up for struggling students, but will also be quick to start a sentence with a, "Listen here, boy…" if proper respect isn't maintained. No matter what my mama says, she has found her purpose as a teacher. She, of all people, knows that her presence and wisdom is needed to serve as an extra mother in an academic setting. She gives it to those kids straight.

From my playing days to now, Mama is a Florida Gator fanatic, yelling at the TV every Saturday, loudly supporting the orange and blue. She is then reserved and reverent on Sunday at her Victory Temple Church of Reconciliation. Mama can be everything to everyone, while remaining 100% true to herself, her faith and her family. I try to be the same way. Balance, even when walking a high wire, is something my mother has always had.

I am in awe of my mama. I always will be. Truth is, there are probably countless sacrifices she has made that I will never know about, likely by her design. In an era of constant promotion and look-what-I-just-did publicity, stunts which have always made me uncomfortable, my mama has saved lives in silence. She never wanted some great reward or public praise, just for her family to be safe and together. One of her favorite sayings is, "If it be the Lord's will." She lives her life that way.

This is how I understood how to not just look the part and sound the part, but to be the part as well. My mama always says keep God first and thank Him for all that you have and all that you are. I continue to try to live up to His and her standards.

Ben Troupe is a mama's boy and that will never change. To some grown men, that may be a slight; to me, it's the ultimate compliment and correction. I celebrate the power of our deep and personal relationship and want to share her way of thinking and living with everyone that I meet. I know the immeasurable value of all that Mama stands for and represents. I know the love that she is so eager to share. Most importantly, I know the person Mama is when people both are and aren't looking, an important distinction in society today. She is the same, regardless.

So much of the good I do comes from my mama and the lifelong lessons she instilled. Through her, I learned to fight and forgive all the same. Both processes remain ongoing.

So much that I experience, see or hear reminds me of my mother. One of the most famous songs from the career of the late legend Tupac Shakur was his personal track "Dear Mama". In it, he said, "I appreciate how you raised me and all the extra love that you gave me," among other authentic and powerful lyrics. I feel more indebted to my mama every day. I see even more magic in her ways as time goes on.

What I owe Mama is nothing less than everything. What she means to me is somehow even more than that.

Paying homage to one of my favorite artists of all-time, I have my own open letter for my mama that I want to share. Though it is for her, specifically, my hope is that she and the world read it with the same respect and admiration. That is a platform this woman has earned. Mama is a person, but a principle, too. I'm sure there are many with similar bonds with certain family or friends. Stories of such love must be shared and celebrated.

Dear Mama,

Thank you for your love, support and faith and the sacrifices you made for me. I thank God everyday for giving you to me and me to you. I could have been anybody's son, but God saw fit to give me the one somebody who would not only give me life but help shape my life as well.

Mama, I am a dreamer and you never killed the dream in me. Mama, I am a creator and you never killed the creativity in me. By always supporting my ideas and ways of doing things, you gave me a sense of purpose. By laughing with me, you gave me a sense of humor. By loving me, you gave me compassion. By never giving up or giving in, you gave me strength. By God being the head of your life, you gave me faith. Mama, you always have something to say before I can even finish my first statement, but that, as frustrating as it can be, is just you being you. Over the years, that has actually paved the way for me to find my voice. You allowed me to make my mistakes.

I know sometimes I am hard to understand, but, still, you just let me be me. You have watched me grow from a boy to a man. You have watched me evolve from who I am to who I am becoming. But most importantly, we have gone from mother and son to best friends. The appreciation and admiration I have for you surpasses time and understanding. You are my girl and a bag of pearls. While there are certain things in life that I question, you taking pride in me and being proud of me is not one of them. A mother's love is rare. A mother's love is pure. A mother's love is uncommon. That is what you are to me, Mama. You are love. You are rare. You are uncommon.

You have always believed in me and, because of that, I believe in myself. You have never allowed me or others to speak negatively or falsely about me. You simply do not play that. Thank you, for no other reason than you are mine and I am yours. You let me know that God doesn't make mistakes and that before I was ever born he knew the mama I would need to give me life and shape my life. All so that I could have the best life. You are the very best. I mean every word. I love you.

Growing up I used to sing all of the time so Mama always thought that I would be a singer. One of my favorite groups is *Boyz II Men.* They have a song called "Mama". My favorite part of the track is when they sing "Loving you is like food to my soul." Mama's love has been my greatest nourishment. This is a woman who never leaves anyone hungry.

WE ALL WE GOT

It is impossible to see me, Ben Troupe, and not see Lucus Troupe, Nikki Bellinger and Carianna Troupe as well. We always have been and, even when we get frustrated with each other, always will be one and the same. Being from Swainsboro, Georgia, family is the starting point for everything that I think and feel. Also, all that I do and pursue. When you address me, you are talking to Lucus, Nikki and Carianna. When you listen to me, you are hearing from each of them, too.

My siblings are each independently original, successful and unique in their own right. They certainly don't need me to highlight them anymore than their own merit already does. Our shared bond is unbreakable and proud.

Much like my relationship with my mother and father, I am not the same man without each of their specific influences on me and my frame of reference. All that I have done has been with Lucus, Nikki and Carianna right there with me.

Lucus will forever be my go-to guy and the man I follow into the future. For as long as I can remember, I have been chasing him. I have looked up to my big brother my entire life and have needed his confidence, fire and protection time and time again. While Lucus is just one year older than me, he has always made it a point to carry all of the weight that comes with being the older brother. Going back to the beginning, he has had my back, has taken the fall for me, has shown me the ropes, has shown me what to do and what not to do, has stood up for me and has always been a shout or a phone call away.

We are quite close in age, but I have always viewed Lucus with the bewilderment of him being a much older man. My personality, especially growing up, was more reserved and shy. That has never been the case with Lucus. His strong will pulled me through some of the toughest times in my life, most notably the move from Swainsboro to Augusta.

As I learned to embrace a more aggressive and competitive side of myself through high school and college football, Lucus was there to encourage me and remind me that I was a Troupe and could do anything. Lucus helped me find my courage.

Every time I put my pads on, my inner-Lucus found a way to come out. And trust me on this, that side of me is one people want no part of. You never mess with Lucus Troupe.

Let me tell you a little more about the man that is the myth. When we were mere grade-schoolers, Lucus took serious offense with a basketball card trade we made with a neighborhood kid. He, upon further review, felt that we had been ripped off and decided that he needed to directly address the situation.

Know this: my brother doesn't go around looking for trouble. He never has. But he will stand up for his friends and family every single time, especially if we, in his opinion, have been slighted. Lucus never started any fights, but he ended all of them. This was even true when he was eleven years old.

Frustrated, Lucus promptly marched back over to the other kid's house, banged on the door and demanded that we all revisit the previous card transaction. Our classmate, unhappy with Lucus showing up again, promptly went and got his dad. My brother, as I knew he would, fearlessly stood his ground and continued to demand that the card be returned.

Looking back on that moment, if that man would have tried Lucus, my brother would have beaten the brakes off of that dude. And he still would have wanted his card back. In that moment, my brother was saying what our great-grandmother Baby Child used to say: "You better find you somebody to play with and if you can't knock 'em out with what you have, pick up something bigger to hit 'em with." Lucus was not there to mess around.

My brother would not leave that front porch, regardless of who came out of that front door. He went and retrieved a large stick to aid his cause when he was told to beat it. I'm not condoning this, but, when the situation boiled over, Lucus ultimately hit the kid with that very stick in the street right in front of his own house. My bolder, older brother was not leaving until he felt like the wrongs against us, involving a special David Robinson card, were corrected. As the dust finally settled, Lucus looked at me when we were running home and said, "it better not be bent, neither."

Years later, as Lucus was having some minor behavioral problems in school, his geometry teacher Mrs. Harris told him in class that she was going to have her husband come down to the school and have a face-to-face talk to him. Lucus calmly stood up, in front of everyone, and un-apologetically told his teacher to bring her little fat hus-band down there and that he was going to get whooped. In that moment, Lucus literally wanted that grown man to come to the school and try him.

In the words of my cousin John-John, "you got to bring some ass to get some."

To know Lucus is to love him and to mess with any-body he loves is just not going to be good for you. I needed that as I grew up without the conviction, often scared and timid, that he clearly had. For stretches of our childhood, Lucus was basically my dad. I think his re-solve, and his quick temper, came from the fact that he knew he sometimes had to be a father to us all. Even if he didn't quite know how. Through everything we experi-enced, Lucus gave it his best and never once backed down from any challenge.

When we first moved to Augusta and learned to navi-gate a new neighborhood, Lucus walked with me every-where I went. He looked out for me. He supported me. He protected me. We lived in Williamsburg Apartments off of Milledgeville Road, then off Davis Road and off Shali-mar Road. That apartment complex is what I remember the most. Each cul-de-sac there was like its own little uni-verse. It was there when I had to navigate through fear for the first time as I didn't know those people and they didn't know me.

There were fights everyday, bloody ones. I kept a low profile and tried to stay out of the way. Lucus, as the older brother, however, had to lead the charge. Even if he was as scared as me, he sure didn't show it. Being John

Troupe's son made Lucus tough as it was. Him navigating those streets made him extra tough. Lucus had to stand tall for both of us. It was him who was often the man of the house and, beyond just that, the man of the neighborhood.

Danger never gave Lucus any doubt, most specifically when he was standing up for me. There is no way I ever could have found my way in Augusta without Lucus and all that he did for me. I needed a big brother and, at times, I needed a dad. Lucus, though barely older than me, gave absolutely all that he had to be both.

Together, we used to work at a car wash and do so for hours on Saturdays. At the end of every shift, he would look at our boss, no matter how much money he gave us, and say, "that's not enough." Before he was even a teenager, Lucus would stand up and demand the best for us. He wouldn't let anyone short him and would never, under any circumstances, let anyone short me. Mama still tells stories of Lucus asking about what and how much I was getting when he was a toddler. He was my protector.

It's no wonder that Lucus joined the United States Marines Corps. His eagerness to serve, though a little misguided as a child, was always there. And Lucus was never one to leave anyone behind. His military career took him across the globe, with his heart and soul going into the unknown with a determined drive to do what was right.

Lucus did a remarkable eight tours of duty overseas, deployments which stretched over a full decade from 2002 -2012. The Marines took him to Afghanistan, Africa, Crete, Egypt, Germany, Iraq, Spain, Souda Bay and the Suez Canal. Freedom, in each location, was his cause. Though the circumstances were obviously more important and widespread, Lucus was simply doing more of what he had always done. He was leading men by his side in the most serious of environments, still standing up for others.

That is the Lucus I have always known, respected and loved. He, not me, is the hero.

A lot of people don't know this about Lucus, but he, built like a bulldog and a workout warrior, was also quite the football player. In some ways, his resume is better than mine. Lucus starred on the All-Marine football team as a strapping younger man, compiling defensive statistics that are hard to even imagine. He even had a tryout with Texas A&M to play linebacker. Another son of John Troupe and another nephew of Robert Troupe, Lucus is of course a great athlete. Just a miniature version.

Speaking of small things, Lucus has my Florida-Georgia Hall of Fame bust somewhere in his closet. Sometimes, I think he thinks it's his face, not mine. Given all he has done and accomplished, it probably should be.

I deeply appreciate the fact that Lucus was never bitter towards me. It couldn't have been easy, especially with what he was doing in work which was actually meaningful, to have dealt with me being a football standout. It was Lucus who held open those doors for me and he never got credit. He also never got jealous. Lucus is everything a brother is supposed to be. I can never be him, but I can acknowledge the reality that Lucus let me be me. That is leadership.

Big Brother,

Thank you for helping me discover who I am. We shared a bedroom for 17 years, yet you always gave me the space to find my authenticity through you living your life your way. I know it may have been difficult at times being the big brother who always got asked about the little brother, but if I didn't have the big brother I had there is no way I would have had the life I did. Thank you for making every environment for me safe.

Lucus' life has taken him to places I can't even find on a globe. And like any brothers, we have had our moments where we have been at odds. But one undeniable truth remains. Like in the movie *The Town*, I can call Lucus and tell him I need him, not tell him why, not tell him where and not tell him who and before I could hang up the phone, he would be in the truck, on the way and ready to do whatever needed to be done. Mess with the little brother, get the big brother to this day.

My entire life, I have chased that legacy. Even as an adult, I went with Lucus to North Dakota, of all places, to do some seasonal work in the coldest place on planet Earth. When I spoke there, my words stopped and turned to ice mid-air. I couldn't breathe, I could barely see and I had to completely redefine my basic understanding of what it meant to be uncomfortable. The cold actually made my bones hurt. Sometimes late at night, when I'm half asleep and sort of dreaming, I still have nightmares of those negative temperature readings and even briefly feel the terrifying frigidity that came with them. North Dakota is no joke.

With that experience, it felt like we were the only two brothers for hundreds of miles; in this case, I'm not talking about siblings.

One of my favorite places to go to this day is the home of my sister Nikki. Anywhere she is becomes a place of laughter and love. Nikki grew up a little bit different than the rest of us, spending most of her life in Augusta. She attended nearby Paine College, where she played softball. Nikki has always been a focused, motivated individual. In some ways, watching her realize her professional goals, Nikki's ability to fearlessly find her way has been a continuation of all of our mother's hard work. Work that, in terms of Mama's direct pursuit of a career, had to be put on hold.

Not only did Nikki graduate from Paine as an accomplished student-athlete, she also earned a Master's Degree from the University of Georgia. Make no mistake about it, through, this girl remains a Florida Gator through and through. Beyond just my time in Gainesville, Nikki, when she was still technically a Bulldog, cried when Tim Tebow failed to convert a game-deciding fourth down run in our 2008 home loss to Ole Miss. There was no need to fret, though, sister. We all know what happened after that game: a finish to the season that Georgia hasn't had since either of us were born.

Nikki is so full of life. This is a girl who once partied with the great T.I. in Gainesville on her first visit to see me at school. This is a woman, as the daughter of John Troupe, who may have the fastests hands in all of east Georgia. Be careful. Most of all, Nikki is a passionate advocate for others, with her work standing as a reflection of both of our parents. Nikki's licensed clinical social work has helped change lives all throughout the Coastal Savannah Riverside District and beyond. She is there for people of all ages and families facing all different types of challenges.

Warm and welcoming, Nikki's beautiful personality is what makes everything she does work so well. She is a fantastic mother and example to my nieces and nephews.

Though, like Lucus and I, capable of getting serious in a hurry if necessary, Nikki is a walking smile. A person with the passion to continue to ask others what more she can do. A mother to four amazing children, Nikki is, in fact, a caretaker to so many more. She has a heart for helping and her light shines on anyone in the family and all that we do. Similar to what Carlos Perez did for me in Gainesville and Erron Kinney did for me in Nashville, Nikki has long been a fixture at my side and in my soul. She taught me that laughter is a key component to my life. Nobody makes me laugh like Nikki.

I'll go ahead and say it: Nikki is the smartest of us all. It is a distinction she has earned. Sometimes when Lucus and I talk to her, we just politely nod and agree, with no real idea of what she is actually talking about. You can't argue with a social worker, anyway. Though younger than us boys, Nikki has still helped raise us in so many ways. Her role as the secondary matriarch alongside Mama, always there to offer Lucus, Carianna and I professional and personal guidance free of charge, has been invaluable. She is another one of the bands that holds us all tightly together.

My admiration for Nikki only grows with time as I continue to measure myself by all that I see in her.

Nikki,

Never, ever change. I do not deserve you as a sister. You are my pride and joy. Thank you for making me laugh. Thank you for showing me how much laughter means to my life. Every time I laugh, a little piece of me is cherishing and appreciating you. Though you will always make me laugh, one of my proudest moments was me crying as I watched you walk across the stage at your graduation from Paine College. In that moment, your life was beginning. Most of all, thank you for Rian, Jalin, Jamie and Julian. Even though I have three children of my own, you gave me four more. I love your children the way you love me.

In terms of our baby sister, Carianna is someone every single one of us needs. A decade or more younger than the rest of us, her innocence and optimism is inspiring. So, too, is her story. Carianna, who my parents raised not long after she was born and later adopted, calls her uncle Daddy and her Daddy uncle. To her, all she sees is love. That perspective is the ultimate example for all of us. Her trust in those around her is reassuring and vesting. She always lets us know how much we all matter, a mindfulness and thankfulness that comes with great power.

Lucus, Nikki and I, all in our own little way, take great pride in feeling like we played a part in raising Carianna. She is our baby.

What Carianna has meant to Mama and Daddy, however, is hard to put into words. Within a span of a few years, Lucus, Nikki and I were all out of the house. While Nikki was close by, she was busy at college. I was obviously out of the state in a very structured environment at Florida. Lucus, most importantly, was soon to be out of the country with the Marines. All of that was a lot for our mother. It would have been for any parent after having a full house for a full generation.

Add in some of our daddy's continued struggles, which were still hit-and-miss, and those natural worries could have come with a constant undertone of unease. With the rest of us suddenly away, Carianna became an even more vibrantly-necessary focal point of Mama's life and love. They developed a special bond. They were there for each other when the rest of us, for various reasons, weren't. Carianna helped our house remain a home.

With her first three children off on their own, Mama got more time to plant a seed and watch it grow with Carianna. And tending to her garden is one of the things Mama does best. Carianna was also extra motivation and another chance for our father. As his fight swayed between incarceration and freedom and addiction and sobriety, with some hope beginning to emerge, Carianna was yet again another front-and-center example of how beautiful life can be. She also gave Daddy another chance at all of the opportunities he did not share with the rest of us.

Daddy was able to do with Carianna some of what he previously missed. Carianna helped make daddy whole once more.

It is simply impossible to tell the Troupe family story without Carianna as she, going all of the way back to that fateful trip to visit family, has been a defining part of both who we all are and what we all represent.

Carianna,

I remember when we first got you to where you are now and all I can say to you is that I am proud of the person you are and I am proud of the person you are becoming. Don't take life too seriously, don't try to have all of the answers, trust your instincts and learn how to dance in the rain.

All of us, through Daddy's missteps and the adversity that we each correspondingly pushed through, found a way forward together. For every team that I have been on, Lucus, Nikki, Carianna and I will always be my original squad. My original crew. Their children are, in a sense, my children. In addition to my beloved three babies Yaya, Mia and B.J., I feel the same adoration for Christian, Jamie, Jalin, Josh, Julian, Kierston, Rian and Triston. We are all one. It remains a daily priority for us to see each other and be around each other as much as at all possible. We simply aren't the same when we are all away.

Love is the ultimate tie that binds. Unlike the laces on my Jordans, which I have to keep loose and let breathe, these double and triple knots are all the hugs that I need.

THE BEN-IONS

I needed the reality check, I really did. And I'm forever grateful for it. Not only was I still a very young man when I entered the NFL, I was distracted, irresponsible and selfish. I was completely lost.

In many ways, I remained motivated by many of the wrong things and interested, infatuated, even, in all that accompanied them. My mindset wasn't an evil one when I got the government stamp of approval for adulthood. I felt like I had a good heart. It was just that very little context came with all that I did or experienced. I wasn't ready for what was coming.

Suddenly, I was rich, relatively famous and had nothing, or nobody, holding me down. There was a freedom to those circumstances, but it was frivolous. Though I may have laughed and smiled, I wasn't always happy. I'm not so sure I even knew how to be at that point. Not searching for meaning, I simply chased what entertained me. The impact of those actions were lost on me at first.

My world centered around me, a gravitational pull which tugged me in all kinds of different directions; Myrtle Beach, South Carolina, included. Life had to teach me how to mature and it did.

In the days leading up to the birth of my first child, a beautiful blessing of a baby boy named Benjamin Zachery, I was getting ready to go on vacation. For the most part, I was hoping to stay there, too. Some friends and I were going to spend a few days on the Grand Strand and, for weeks, I had quietly been hoping that B.J., as we call him, would be born on any other weekend. How selfish was that?

As we were making plans to get settled in and making plans to party, plans quickly changed. B.J.'s mother, a lovely lady named Alicia, was down in Jacksonville, Florida, soon to go into labor.

Not far from where I played a number of football games and made the biggest catch of my life, I was not yet there as the biggest moment of my life was about to make everything else a mere footnote. Yards, no matter how important, will never compare to baby steps. While everyone else will associate me with Jacksonville for a play I made, I will always think about the city for a date I almost didn't.

On May 21st, 2009, I woke up in a hospital in Jacksonville with every intention of Alicia and I soon welcoming our son into the world. I asked the doctor, looking him square in the face, if we were having a baby that night. He said no. Being the person that I was at the time, I got in my car, drove to Swainsboro, got my friends together and headed to Myrtle Beach. All while Alicia and her mother remained in the hospital.

A few hours out from the coast, my worst fear happened; Mrs. Juanita, Alicia's mother, called me and asked me where I was. Though scared, I told her the truth. She explained that Alicia was going into labor. As bad as it sounds and as bad as it was, I was honestly hoping that would not be the case yet.

That was the first time Alicia's mother told me she was disappointed in me. And she was right. I was disappointed in me, too. Alicia had gone through the entire pregnancy by herself and all they were asking was for me to make sure that I was going to be there for the birth of my son.

When I got to Myrtle Beach, I went straight to the airport and flew right back to Jacksonville. God gave me the power of perspective through the gift of life. Call it dumb luck or divine intervention, but in the hours between the day-before and the day-of, I did make it to the hospital on a last-minute, just-in-time flight. I'd like to say, speeding somewhere through the heavens, that I had a complete revelation, but I didn't.

Somewhere between excitement and nervousness, guilt and uncertainty, however, I did have at least a brief moment of clarity. I realized that I was having a child; I don't want to say I was becoming a father, because I wasn't yet. I had no idea what that really meant.

I did finally know that I had to be there and be there for both my son and his mother. In a strange way, I was happy to just be at the hospital. I had never been involved with anything like that before or anything of much significance at all. There was so much going on, with Alicia's parents there and the various medical tests and schedules, the vast majority of which I had nothing to do with. It was a lot to take in and I wasn't even doing anything.

Part of me felt detached, actually. My son was being born and I was very much concerned for his health, but I had not shouldered any of the burden leading up to his birth and I didn't know how to suddenly snap my fingers and, poof, become more involved. It's awful to admit now, but, in my misguided youthful perspective, I kind of felt like I was doing my part. It goes without saying that I wasn't.

B.J. deserved more from me and so did Alicia. I may have been where I needed to be physically, but I was not where I needed to be mentally or as a man. Nowhere even close. I flew in for the birth, was genuinely proud, smiled and took some pictures, then flew back to South Carolina not long after B.J. was born. He even remained in the ICU for a few days after I was gone. It hurts me to even think about that.

In review, part of one day was what I gave the most important day of my life. For that, I apologize to my son, Alicia, Mrs. Juanita, Mr. Lloyd and God Almighty.

My intent was not to disrespect the moment or the many involved. I was not the same person then. My frame of reference was that of a child's, all while I should have been responsible for one. I hate that I thought and acted how I did. Though those are precious moments I can never get back, I take some solace in the fact that they did, as I continued to replay them in my mind for years, help change my outlook to all that is truly important.

While he was still just opening his eyes, B.J. changed the way I saw the world and did so by barely being around me at all.

We call B.J. "Ben Junior", with him being named after me. It should honestly be the other way around as who I was meant to be came after him. B.J. is still creating the new me. B.J. is still helping me become the man who I am now and the man I always thought I could be. I will always see the real me, the me I can be proud of, through

B.J. My son should be introduced before me, a deference he has earned.

When I think about B.J., I am truly humbled. He, and the circumstances around his birth, came at a crossroads in my life. God used B.J. to change me for the better. Without my son, I never could have achieved all that I have. Without my son, I might not have any real achievements at all. Everything I do and continue to do is so that he knows what is possible. My work isn't just for B.J., it is because of him.

Each time B.J. calls or texts, the name "B.J. the Prince" pops up on my phone. He is real royalty, so much more worthy of any fine cloth than his father. B.J. represents hope and change, love and purity. Whenever I hear stories of people overcoming adversity or learning from their past, I think about my son and his impact on me.

I also think, unmistakably, about my daddy. We are three different men now part of one unbreakable bond. None of us would be the same without each other. Each of our experiences, as painstaking as they may have been at times, have made us stronger. When I tell B.J. stories about my pops, I want him to know that he can and should be proud of his grandfather. That his grandfather is an overachiever. That his daddy is an overachiever. Because of who he is and how greatly he has changed me, my son can now be proud of his daddy as well.

You would have thought that when B.J. was born, that old, selfish, immature me would have immediately faded away. It didn't. Over the years though, through trials and tribulations, that version of me is now a former one. It took some time, but I owe so much of my personal transformation to Him and him. Beyond B.J. being my first-born, he will always bring a smile to my face because of all that he did and is still doing for me. In him and the Lord, I was born again.

I pray that God will give me the time to continue to be not only a better father but also B.J.'s friend. That was certainly the case with me and my daddy.

B.J. redefined love for someone who had always been a little bit scared of it, a little unwilling to trust it. He taught me how to see my actions beyond just myself. He taught me responsibility. B.J. also taught me accountability and accepting my role as a father, even if my actions didn't show it right away. In a time where I was jumping between the who, what, when, where and whys of the world, he provided the answers to all of my questions. B.J. revealed my true character, which I didn't initially have. He also helped me better understand my own father and my relationship with him.

Something I couldn't do on my own, B.J. helped me learn to respect all that was around me, myself included. When it comes to my son, I still struggle to find the words.

B.J.,

First, I just want to say thank you. Thank you for being my son. Thank you for giving me a reason to grow up. Thank you for being my why. I want to apologize for not being there for you the way I needed to be and wanted to be. I'm sorry for not understanding and embracing my role of being your daddy and you being my son. I was im-

mature. I was selfish. I was inconsiderate. I was a fool. I pray that you can forgive me and that God gives me time to show you who I am and gives you time to get to know who your daddy is. Who your daddy really is. B.J., you are my legacy. You are my prince. You are the best and greatest part of me, you and your sisters.

B.J., thank you for always loving me, my past, my faults and my imperfections. Thank you, Alicia, for naming B.J. after me. Son, always know that my love for you has never wavered, even when my presence or actions made it seem differently. I want you to know that you are my heart, my smile, my joy, my life, my everything. I will never do anything in this life better than you and your sisters. You are my masterpiece. Thank you for just being you. Thank you for being mine. Thank you for being my son.

Most importantly, thank you Benjamin Zachary Troupe for being a gift from God.

What does a father say to a son? I simply say: B.J. I love you to the moon and back. You and your sisters are my greatest accomplishments and I am humbled to be your daddy.

If my son was my introduction to real life, my two daughters, Mia and Iara, who we call Yaya, are my gorgeous reminders. Together, the three of them form the exact cadence of my heartbeat. My one pulse comes straight from those three children, each of them extraordinary extensions of whatever good is or ever has been in me. The abundancy God has given me knows no bounds.

They are all so amazing and unique in their own distinct ways. A look into the eyes of Mia or Yaya is a glimpse into all that is genuine in the world. Both have laughs that travel at the speed of light and grins that immediately brighten a room. It's impossible to see either of them, glowing faces hidden amongst heads full of frizzy hair, and not feel uplifted. They are invigorating and refreshing. While B.J. remains my steady Sunday morning, Mia and Yaya come with all the feels of waking up the morning before.

Born in the same month, but not twins, my girls share a common energy. Like with my mama, there is a light to both of them that is illuminating and inspiring and not just for me. I see a new horizon through them that I never could have imagined or formed on my own. Though I have always respected women, feeling even an extra obligation to honor them because of my mother and sister, I never really saw the world through their perspective until I started seeing my daughters in every woman I met.

I have become more aware and understanding of the plight women never ask for, yet almost-always have to deal with. There are so many assumptions, biases, difficulties and extra adversities that women, even as young girls, must work their way through. My outlook quickly became dramatically more reverent. It remains that way. God bless women.

I'm absolutely honored to have girls. There is true joy in raising girls and, at least for me, there was a profound awakening that occurred along the way. I'm so appreciative of how Mia and Yaya have molded me into a better man. They, to this day, help me see every woman as someone else's daughter, a revelation that has helped me approach every day more as I should.

It's hard to completely appreciate a woman until you love a little girl. Loving two of them, my heart will always be full.

A few weeks older than her sister, Mia is an unapologetically authentic pursuer of all of her wildest imaginations. She is raw and pure, direct and passionate and won't waste her or your time patronizing others with a compromised or hesitant opinion. Maybe she gets that from her mama and my mama. Mia is confident in her beliefs, captivating fixtures which include family and fun. I call her my "Fire Rose", full of sass and vigor. Not only does Mia know what she likes, she is eager to tell you all about it as well.

What is so amazing is that there are things that Mia does that are exact replications of a younger me. She stands as close as she can to the television while watching it. I still do, too. She will play, full of energy, by all herself. I am sometimes at my most content in time spent alone. She sings all of the time. I used to as a young boy. Unlike me as a child, Mia already knows who she is.

Mia will study you, up close and from afar, and form a working perspective that immediately responds to any and all new information. Her mind is like a computer, though her emotions are as intimately personal as it gets. Maybe that's all women and I'm simply still learning.

Regardless of who she is around, Mia is colorful and outgoing. Almost like a step into a classic candy store. She is expressive and thoughtful, singing, beautifully, in any environment, at the top of her lungs. That joy, even in the simplest of moments, is who she is. The apprehension that might slow even the most confident of voices in new or uncomfortable settings is an opportunity that Mia jumps at every time. She sounds like ice cream tastes. Whether her ringing voice or random insights, Mia leaves little room for interpretation.

A deep thinker, Mia loves to create, from cooking to baking to playing with dolls. Mia is herself all of the time. That, above anything else, is my girl. Not just making the most of any moment, Mia is every moment. She has the personality to make time slow down or stand still.

Mia once held a joyous makeshift concert for her grandparents as we waited on my brother to bring us a key to his house. She did so right on his front porch, without any planning or preparation. Everywhere, for Mia, is a stage. My daddy still says that was some of the most beautiful singing that he has ever heard.

I thank Mia's mother Stephanie for always reminding my daughter that she never needs to be anything more than just herself. Nothing could be more true.

Mia,

Thank you for being such a kind and beautiful soul. Thank you for giving Daddy time to get out of my own way so that I could be the daddy for you I always knew I could be and the daddy you deserve and need me to be. I have a lot of work to continue on this journey of being a daddy, a willing daddy, a vulnerable daddy, a loving daddy, but most importantly your daddy.

Make sure you never stop being you because in the midst of you being you, you helped Daddy see and become himself. Mia, you are my Fire Rose. You are what gives me hope, energy and enthusiasm to keep going. You are mine and I am yours. We are stuck with each other for life and you're not getting rid of me. I wouldn't have it any other way.

My frame of reference with Yaya is somewhat different. Unlike with B.J. and Mia, I raised Yaya in a traditional family setting. Though I am thankful for all I have learned from raising my previous two children and obviously adore every second I have had with them, I was with Yaya from conception to delivery. I was there from infancy up through milestones that I will always remember.

Some of the things I got wrong with B.J. and Mia, I was able to get right with Yaya. At least I hope and pray so. Part of my daddy's story resonates with me here.

Watching Yaya transition through the various phases of her childhood gave me a more dynamic understanding of the role of the father and the multi-faceted meaning behind the relationship a dad can and should have with his kids. Though Yaya was my third child, I was far from an expert in how to care for any of them.

I leaned on a woman who had long settled and guided me, my ex-wife Maria. It may not have worked out with her long-term, but Maria offered me the stability I needed. She showed me how to settle into a regular routine post-football. Family was how Maria helped me find my way in a trying time in my life.

We weren't ever perfect together, but we did love each other and make it a priority to raise our daughter in a nurturing, positive environment. Yaya was made and raised in love.

The family I had with Yaya is one that I will always hold dear. Maria and I had some great times together, memories which our daughter will always be a leading part of. Our house was open and fun, with friends and family visiting from miles around. It was often a loud and boisterous place, folks coming and going and laughing and smiling. An unassuming little woman was almost-always quietly front and center; and I'm not talking about Maria or our baby.

I will never forget Maria's late mother Nona, a strong and stoic lady who was full of stories and strength. While she, a native of Peru, barely spoke broken English, her presence was always pronounced. In addition to being a tireless caregiver for Yaya, she brought culture and cour-age into our home. Nona would do anything for family, a notion which meant a lot to me.

Through our commonalities, I started to better respect the trials and tribulations of those I didn't necessarily know. I stopped being so presumptive. I started listening more, even when I wasn't quite sure what was being said. Maria embodies so many of her mother's endearing traits, as do her brothers Tony, Carlo and Luigi. Tony always made me laugh and was so optimistic about the future. Carlo, who helped me understand the artistry that is act-ing, regularly encouraged me. I still appreciate those guys.

My marriage was an experience with ups and downs. It is one I am better for, however. It is one I would not be the same without. I have no regrets.

Maria,

Thank you for showing me how to be fearless in my approach, fearless in my way of being, fearless in general. Thank you for being who you are, which gave me permission to be who I am. Thank you for your strength. Thank you for your vulnerability. Thank you for showing me that only a select few in life get to truly know who we actually are. Thank you for the intangibles you gave me that I will use for a lifetime. Most of all, thank you for our little girl. Without her, I am not the father I am. And without you, I never break out of my shell. True love is a real thing, but unconditional love is an even greater thing.

Like her mommy, daddy and so many of her ancestors, Yaya is also a proud and beaming original. She, from karate to soccer to swimming, got my athletic genes and, fret not "Gator Nation", my jean shorts as well. Yaya is active and engaged, an already orange-and-blue competitor who is at her best in the spotlight. That stage, for her, is under the sun. Yaya thrives outside, a Florida girl who has grown up stretching towards the sky in the dunes along Space Coast. Like the sand on the tide-tinted beaches where she runs, the complexion of Yaya's skin sometimes changes after days out and about.

No matter where she is, Yaya, born at Stanford Hospital in northern California, learning to walk in foothills around Atlanta and having started grade-school in the suburbs of New Jersey, is my island girl. At home or in the big city, she is always looking outdoors; endless opportunities are what she sees.

Though she may never fully understand it, Yaya set the stage for it all. She gave me purpose. She helped me fit and understand my description more completely and become a better father to all of my children.

Yaya,

Thank you for showing me the way. Thank you for showing me what it is to be a daddy. Thank you for filling in the blanks where I had so many questions. Thank you for being the answered prayer of God in Him sending you to me. You taught me accountability. You taught me responsibility. You taught me humility. You taught me how to love unconditionally. You gave me parenthood and an understanding of it in a way that I don't think I would have realized without you. You saved my life. Your fearlessness and outgoing personality are as beautiful to watch as your face is to gaze upon.

Yaya, I'm a real daddy because of you. I'm the real me because of you. I am deeply indebted to you simply for you being you. You are my Yaya-Mac-Fafa for life. My girl and a bag of pearls with curls. You, just like your brother and sister, are my heart, my smile, my joy, my life, my everything.

Each of my experiences with my children have made me try to do and be more, a process that will never end. I am far from a perfect father, but I am a persistent one. All three of my kids will always know how much I love them, how much they mean to me and how profoundly they have impacted me for the better. It is my mission to make sure my children have absolutely no doubt, both in terms of how special they are as people and how meaningful they are to me. I love each of them equally and unrelentingly forever.

Anything I was or ever will be comes far after a title that I have been blessed to be called by three different joys of my life: "Daddy."

I still am learning. I'm constantly striving to be a better, more complete father and some of my most sincere conversations I have now are with fellow parents in search of fellowship towards a common good.

I champion men like Ben Watson, who I competed with at the 2004 NFL Combine, for his transparency in talking about how important parenting can be and for sharing his experiences with others. We, as athletes, as men and as people, have to continue to shine a light on the real depth and value of all of our contributions. Whenever I hear men, in my case, talk about the challenges and thrills of parenting, I make it a point to listen and learn. Nothing we do in life will be more important. Improvement has to be our constant goal.

Clearly, I have made countless mistakes with B.J., Mia and Yaya. I still do. But I have not accepted those missteps as my forever path. I march forward and, for my kids, I will always go the extra mile. My whole life has been measured by height and weight and speed and strength, but I find vulnerability to be the ultimate ability. As a society, we must make it a point to share our feelings with one another, especially as it pertains to the next generation. There is no greater responsibility.

I was not the player at the start of my career that I was years down the line. I constantly took everything I learned and applied it to my future. I reinvented myself with nuance and subtlety. The end result was a constantly evolving product, one where I got better with experience. I became a veteran. Just like my mama, I simply refuse to settle.

My training as a parent, from self-evaluation to redefining my skills, continues in the same way. As my children have grown, my perspective has, too. I will never be a finished product, only one most-reflective of the information and opportunity to date. Once I rest, whether as a player, a parent or a person, my progress also stops. Both my mama and my daddy stand as testaments to that process.

I will always be the person I am and the person I am becoming. I owe that growth to my kids. When people say leave the world better than you found it, with B.J., Mia and Yaya, I can say I have.

UNCONDITIONAL

It was the spring of 2014. My father, finally making some significant progress in his fight against addiction, had just moved back in at home. Daddy and I were driving around Swainsboro, something I still like to do, riding right past City Hall on what seemed like another regular hot-and-sticky south Georgia night. I had heard from my mama and had just gathered on my own given all that Daddy had recently been through, that he had been doing a lot of thinking, praying and reflecting about all of his trials and tribulations. I certainly had been.

Through it all, I still wasn't quite sure how to feel about my father. I didn't know how he felt about me or what the future of our often-tenuous relationship might hold. So many emotions were barred up inside of me: anger, disappointment, frustration, pain and sadness. Years of not understanding.

As a grown adult in my early 30s, I still had a deep yearning to grow closer to this mystery man. I needed to know why he said some of the things he said and why he did some of the things he did. Why he often left our mother and us kids alone as he lived his own secret life in the shadows. Even then, I didn't know if I could get past it all. I couldn't make it all make sense.

I wanted to angrily grab this stranger and warmly hug my daddy all at once. I wanted to wrestle us both away from our shared past and rip down any of the cumbersome walls that might continue to be standing between us. I wasn't quite sure how. I have always had an angry fascination for deconstruction, an urge to rip everything around me to shreds. That night I did so while never taking my eyes off the road.

While we had obviously been through a lot together, Daddy and I, we had never really talked about it. We had never really discussed much of anything. We lived life, but rarely shared more than simple small talk or circumstantial conversation. For the most part growing up, we didn't say, "I love you", didn't physically embrace, didn't discuss the birds and the bees and largely avoided the tough talks.

With Daddy away for long stretches, we simply didn't have many of the milestone moments that naturally open the door for those opportunities. Neither of us knew how to force the issue.

The older we both got, the more awkward it naturally became. The more I learned, the more awkward it deliberately became. The further apart we grew, the harder it became to even start to figure out how to go back. Where was the road to recovery? I didn't know how to talk to my father about what I knew and what I didn't know. I honestly felt uncomfortable trying to suddenly foster an intimate bond that never really existed in the first place.

In terms of my relationship with my daddy, I genuinely had more questions than answers. Way more. We weren't that far removed from him randomly showing up at my house in Nashville and asking for a car. I wasn't certain of what he might do, much less how he might feel.

Not that long before our breakthrough, there was very nearly a breaking point.

In one of the lowest points of my father's life, one of his last outbursts before complete reconciliation, he busted out the windows in my mama's car and in my car. He also made some unacceptably vile threats to my mother on her voicemail, all of which rightfully got my daddy arrested once again. He was out of control and needed to be detained.

Mama and I met with the sheriff and had a heart-to-heart. It was a critical but uncomfortable conversation. Daddy had wronged us, so we were directly involved in conversations about his future. I still didn't want the man who birthed me to be in jail for a long period of time. I was angry, frustrated and scared yet again. That said, I didn't want to play lawyer and didn't want to slam the door by locking Daddy's cell shut for who knows how long. In this situation, my opinion mattered. God gave me the grace to help me understand that my daddy needed to be punished and helped and forgiven all at once.

Weighing it all, I realized I needed to address my daddy man-to-man. After some serious reflection, I went to the jailhouse to meet and talk with my father. I had not had many deep discussions with my father before, especially as an adult, so I had no idea how all of this was going to go. This was the first time I had ever visited him in jail by myself. We were both standing on the same line in the sand. This one just happened to be separated by plexiglass.

I was very nervous. While I knew I wasn't in the wrong, part of me still felt like I was because I was confronting my own pops. I had to show my daddy that I was upset, but that I was still there for him. Honestly, I needed to understand why he had been acting the way he was. What was he thinking and feeling? Violence was unacceptable, especially towards our mother. Within that understanding, I was also there to help him get better.

If I'm being honest, I was trying to help myself get better, too. I had never confronted hardly anything in life, especially my father. Mama was still hoping and praying. I was still learning.

.When I entered the seemingly-hopeless facility, a female officer of the prison walked up to me and said, "You're John's boy, I remember you when he was holding you in his arms." It was a full circle experience as I had been in facilities my whole life. I had never been in one quite like this, however, and that moment nearly stopped me in my tracks. .

I approached the line of demarcation not knowing what to expect. What I experienced was something I never could have imagined, something that shocked and shook me. The man who gave me life could not look me in the eyes. Forever a strong and brawny figure, Daddy was lifelessly slumped to the side in devastating disgust and shame. He would not turn his face towards mine.

To me, my daddy's most meaningful transformation started right there. He saw the light by refusing to look into it.

The Lord gave me the strength to tell him that I was not there to disrespect him. I told him that I was there because I was his son. Right there, in a room with bare walls and peeling-paint, everything got stripped down to the basics. Any and every pretense of bravado or personal stature was irrelevant and meaningless. All pride was absent.

Unbridled fear was on display at every turn. Our backs were against the wall, literally and figuratively.

It was there that both our respective personas faded. I don't think that either one of us ever intentionally put up a facade. I actually think we each perceived the other in ways that weren't real or reflective. My daddy, not knowing me as he should have, often chose to see me, even vilify me, as a famous football player who was largely off in my own glamorous world. He sometimes felt that way even as I was inside his own home. I often saw him as a man who wouldn't, for whatever reason, get right. Someone who avoided the people and places that loved him, forgave him and always treated him the best.

Deep in our hearts, we both knew those assumptions weren't entirely true. But we desperately needed more confirmation in our own personal ways. Misconceptions have to be torn down with purpose. Otherwise they will only slightly fade with time.

There were blanks left to be filled in. Those who are fortunate enough to have life's full phraseology might not fully appreciate what it's like when those most important words aren't ever there. Use a simple thought exercise for example. Take two following statements and compare them to one another: "my father and I love each other" vs "my father and I ___ each other." Even if you are pretty sure what the missing word is, it isn't the same to merely read those two different distinctions, much less actually live them.

There is an obvious void when feelings aren't expressed, one that can be the starting point for so much more that is broken and hollow. It can be the little things in life that make the biggest difference. Daddy was finally on his way to making up his mind to truly want to be able to break free from the chains of addiction and abuse. He triumphed with the support of faith and family, a realization we all knew he was capable of. We then needed our father to be direct with the hidden details that were still remaining.

For my mother, Lucus, Nikki, Carianna and I, we didn't need to "think" anymore. We needed to "know".

One seemingly regular night, the excruciating boiling point of three decades of dark doubt and uncertainty were suddenly and stunningly overcome in a matter of mere moments. My father, shaken by his most recent mistakes and how I, in his mind, responded, completely broke down. The proverbial dam collapsed with him. From there, the words flowed like rushing waters.

All that I had so long wanted to hear, all that I had so long wanted to say, burst out into the open like piercing sunlight across a dark horizon. The words came in an all-out sprint, running right past all of the bad memories and lonely nights. Fears were restored to faith.

Daddy started and could not stop. I, waiting on these explanations for a lifetime, didn't want him to. Every phrase my father uttered was comforting, empowering and soothing. Both stubborn men in our own rights, we were immediately transformed and inspired. I felt like I had found my conviction. It was like we were meeting for the very first time.

I saw my daddy, him calmly sitting in my passenger's seat, finally take the wheel. Driving on an all-too-familiar road both of us had been down thousands of different times, we, somehow, finally, found our way.

Daddy, out of nowhere and over and over again, told me just how much he loved me. He, for the first time ever, explained to me exactly how much I meant to him and how I had always been a leading part of his life. My father took me back to where it all started, sharing specific memories of he and I that I didn't know were anywhere in his mind. He took the time to tell me how proud he was of me and, just as importantly, to explain why.

Finding the words with just the flickers from the dash and the gleam of the headlights humming in the dusk of night, Daddy apologized for all that he did to me and our family, painstakingly sharing how he wasn't himself in those stretches. How he didn't mean some of the hurtful things he did say and how he wished he said some of the caring things he didn't.

Humbly, my father spoke in adulation about my mother. He offered indebted testimony of how her unconditional and unfathomable grace changed his life. All of this, for me, was an utter revelation. For a generation, I felt like I really didn't know my own father. At times, it was a downright devastating disconnect. All of the pieces were now being put back together.

These interactions were my first truly personal conversations with the man I had always seen myself in. I had my daddy back. We made up for lost time with every mile.

You would think that what happened that night would have taken me back. Back to moments where I was in desperate need of my father's teachings and guidance. Back to when I needed his discipline and direction. Back to when we all needed Daddy to help make ends meet or hold the rest of us together through home moves and job changes. Back to when Lucus, ready or not, had to be the man of the house. Back to when I didn't know what tomorrow would hold. Back to when I was celebrating some of the biggest moments of my life and my own father wasn't there to share them with me.

Back to when he, and all of us visiting him, were so often imprisoned.

Our dialogue, somewhat surprisingly, didn't take me there. I was suddenly excited about the future. The present immediately became an unexpected gift. All of the ways my heart and soul were stuck long in the past, my mind was instantly fixed on the here and now. I heard what I needed to hear. I saw what I needed to see. Above all else, I felt what I needed to feel.

There is no way my daddy can make up what he did to me or the rest of my family. Especially our mama. None of us, however, will ever know the misfortunes we may have knowingly or unknowingly inflicted upon others. To be fair, there is no way I can fully appreciate what he was going through, either. I think sometimes, in life, people are understandably so hurt when they feel wronged that the standard they set for forgiveness is unrealistic.

I was never wanting or expecting my daddy to provide some PowerPoint presentation of all that happened or to shower me with gifts or praise. I just wanted him to be honest with me and to let me know what was truly in his heart. I didn't need my father to be anything special. I just needed him to be my daddy. That night, in every way possible, he was. He has been ever since.

God is the only one who can give time. Know this, He can give it back, too. Daddy is a living example. After years of walking the path of the disillusioned, he now walks by faith. While much of his trek has been one he chose to walk alone, Daddy's turn is one others can and should follow. The burden is never too great. The cost is never too much. The time is never too late. The reasons are never too big or too small. The risk, when finding your way, is always worth it.

Daddy is a miracle. God's miracle. Mama's miracle. Our miracle. My miracle.

Even when I thought I hated my father, I still loved him. And I, like all sons, always strived for his approval. After that evening, my eyes opened up to all that he is and almost-certainly has, at least way down in the depths of his soul, always been. In that car, we weren't an athlete and an inmate or an old man and a young man. We were just a father and a son. We were two daddys embracing the blessing of it all.

An unplanned, unprompted conversation became my paradigm shift. It was a common moment between uncommon men.

I have always seen myself as the person I am and the person I am becoming. After our crossroads conversation, I whole-heartedly gave my daddy that same benefit of the doubt. Beyond that, I quickly started to further appreciate his vitally important role as a grandfather, the lessons and love he could share with my children. They are, in every possible way, better with him as a leading figure in their lives.

So are the countless young people in the Swainsboro and south Georgia communities my daddy now mentors.

In the same streets he used to run, Daddy now walks with his head held high. He still goes back to jail, but, this time, to share wisdom and words of encouragement. I am honored to be by his side.

Daddy,

I have always wanted to be just like you. I thought you were the biggest, strongest and best man in the world. I wanted to walk like you. I wanted to talk like you. I wanted to have the same mannerisms as you. I wanted to be built like you. I wanted to have facial hair like you. Most importantly, I wanted to be celebrated like you. Loved like you. I wanted people to love being around me like they do you. I wanted to breathe life and energy into anyone and everything that came into contact with me like you. I wanted to impress and be impressive like you. I wanted to be you.

I wanted you to light up when talking about me. I wanted you to tear up when thinking about me. I wanted you to be proud of me and be proud that I am your son. Daddy, there were times that I needed you that you weren't there. There were times that I needed your advice and you weren't there to give it. There were times that your presence alone was all I needed for my day and my life to feel better. Daddy, you let me know that time is precious and that love should be unconditional.

Daddy, you taught me that even the strong can be weak and even the very best can experience the very worst. You taught me that it takes a man to understand a man. You taught me that doing the right thing is not easy, but it is the right thing to do. Daddy, you taught me that if you get knocked down eight times that you get up nine. You taught me perseverance. You taught me what overcoming is.

You taught me a lot of things, but the best thing you did for me is you made it so I don't have to wonder if you are proud of me anymore and that you love and wish nothing but the best for me. Mama told me that you told her that when it comes to me that when I hurt you hurt. You also told her that when it comes to me that you think I can do anything.

Daddy, you saved my life with a simple conversation and a few simple words. I will never stop wanting to impress you like a little boy saying, "Daddy, look what I just did," or, "look what I can do."

Daddy, thank you for being my daddy. Thank you for being my friend. Thank you for the tough times. Thank you for the rough times. Thank you for being a shining example of what never giving up or giving in looks like. Thank you for the lessons.

Thank you for you. You have always and will forever be my superman without the cape.

My life is a byproduct of the power and persistence of those who showed me the way. Around the country in a dream that went beyond my wildest imaginations, to back home again, my foundation, like Mama alone with us kids, never left.

As a young man, I was able to experience things most only see in the movies. I spent an afternoon at the house of the legendary Rohan Marley, Bob's son. I went to a party with Tom Cruise. I even shook hands with Presidents George Bush and George W. Bush before one of my games. Through it all, I remained a small town boy yearning for the love of my mama and daddy.

I will always be Swainsboro, Georgia. I will always be warm food on a moist paper plate. I will always be a smiling face in a church parking lot. I will always be rain on an old tin roof. I will always be the leftover juice in a can of tiny sausages. I will always be a pair of wrinkled jean shorts. I will always be a pair of fresh Jordans. I will always be a crisp, clean flatbill Atlanta cap. I will always be bright orange and royal blue. I will also always be smurf blue. I will always be a two-bedroom apartment at the Village in Gainesville. I will always be a moment in time in Jacksonville. I will always be a group pick-up order at *Swett's Restaurant* in Nashville. I will always be paying the tab.

I will always be a proud and beautiful black man. I will always be standing alongside our military while kneeling in reflection as well. I will always appreciate and understand the struggle. I will always be an advocate. I will always be a volunteer. I will always hold hands with my brothers and sisters of color. I will always encourage everyone to speak up. I will always tell people that Black

Lives Matter. I will always be pro-black and unapologetically black.

I will always be a 6'5" imposing threat to some. I will always be someone who has to earn outsiders' trust. I will always be the son of a black man who spent time in prison. I will always be the stereotypes others choose to see. I will always be the space-between when people move a step or two to the side. I will always be a nervous soul when pulled over by police with my children in the backseat. I will always be a person of color working to change false narratives. I will always be someone who wants more for people who look like me. I will always, whether I choose to be or not, be a myth-killer. I will always use my voice to speak for the voiceless. I will always use my influence to influence.

I will always be more than an athlete. I will always be a man of God. I will always be kicking it with Titus Peeples, Ben Hall and Troy Fleming. I will always be a two-man Marine Corps with my brother Lucus. I will always be a walk on the beach with B.J., Mia and Yaya. I will always be a house full of nieces and nephews. I will always be a Sunday afternoon with Cora Bell Williams, Nelowese Edwards, Mollie Troupe, Clifford Troupe and James Edwards. I will always be the people who came before me. I will always be standing on their shoulders.

I will always be Cheryl Denise and John Wesley. Through it all, I will always be myself. I will always be the person I am, the person I am becoming and the person I am unbecoming. I will always be uncommon.

I hope our nation will be as well. As horrors have overtaken the headlines pertaining to hate, racial injustice, inequality and police brutality, it's long past time for all of us to take a good, long look in the mirror. We may not like what we see. We shouldn't, in fact. From the unfathomable tragedy of a young black man killed while jogging through a neighborhood not far from my home to the countless stories that we all see on the news, the realities are overwhelming.

Now is the time for change. Now is the time for progress. Not just words, but actions. We owe it to ourselves and our country. Most importantly, we owe it to each other. It's not about what you are willing to do, but the fact that you are willing at all; willing to be uncomfortable, willing to be unpopular and willing to be uncommon.

Our leaders should be here to support everyone. We need systems in place that do the same. The problem is: we don't realize that we are all leaders. The question is: who are you leading? We must be able to ask the question and answer it alike. America doesn't just belong to the rich and the powerful. America belongs to the least amongst us. America belongs to those who get looked over, passed over and those who have never been a priority.

Until America does right by all people, our full potential will never be realized. That's the thing about the American dream; it isn't always the same reality. I love this country. So much so that I will hold it to the highest of standards.

My heart beats with love for all of the selfless advocates who have and are making a difference in the modern civil rights movement. The sacrifices made by these courageous individuals cannot be appreciated enough and will hopefully be emulated and seen as the example rather than the exception. We all must learn to lend a hand and not only an opinion. We are who we have been waiting for; so what are you waiting for? The world is changing. The country is changing. We must lead that change. We get to fight everyday to ensure that the direction remains forward.

The great Martin Luther King, Jr. said to lead from where you are standing. I am standing tall. I am standing firm. I am standing for us.

Being black in America isn't easy. I believe being black is a privilege in its own right and I take so much pride in that fact. I love being black. I love being me. We are all kings and queens.

The United States is supposed to come with opportunity for all. There should not be two Americas, but one equal in grand design. For many, however, the American Dream is nothing more than a distant bedtime story. Alarms are going off. Loudly. It's time we wake up and stay up.

It's time we demand more, both of ourselves and our nation. It's time we make society better, by working on ourselves and our communities first. My pledge is to positively impact as many people as I can. With my speaking, my non-profit organization, my volunteer work and my mentoring, I am here for others. I am here for young people.

I will never stop fighting for the underserved and overlooked. I will continue to push through with the lofty goal of bringing everyone else with me. Bettering himself, his family and his neighborhoods, my daddy sure did.

Different from my mama, Daddy is a leader in his own way. Much like he previously deserved to be punished, he now also deserves to be praised. Daddy paid a deep debt to society and, though prison may not be the rehabilitation some make it out to be, perspective certainly can be.

Together, my parents are the epitome of all that is possible. They, at an early age, took hands and took on the world. Life responded, as it has a tendency to do, with every possible adversity, hell and hate included. Through pain few will ever experience, a promise, one from above and one from within, has come with everlasting life.

There are signs of progress everywhere. It's up to us to build on the framework that is already in place. God has given us the tools. Potential lies within everyone, even those we or society may forget. Never can we, individually or collectively, give up the fight for the greater good. It won't be easy, but we must always fight for people. We must always fight for right. Out there is hope. Out there is truth. Out there is the desire for the unrealistic.

Out there is an uncommon version of ourselves and our world; one that is still unfinished. A simple drive through the country is sometimes all you need to find it.

CPSIA information can be obtained
at www.ICGtesting.com
Printed in the USA
BVHW071122140921
616731BV00002B/45

9 781736 667286